Fight AIDS!

How
Activism, Art,
and Protest Changed
the Course of a Deadly
Epidemic and Reshaped a Nation

FIGHT AIDS!

Michael G. Long

NORTON YOUNG READERS
AN IMPRINT OF W. W. NORTON & COMPANY
INDEPENDENT PUBLISHERS SINCE 1923

*To all the people with AIDS
who took the placebo*

Note to Readers: *Fight AIDS!* is a work of nonfiction. Certain names, dialogue, and potentially identifying characteristics of individuals have been changed, and some scenarios have been reconstructed or revised.

Copyright © 2025 by Michael G. Long

All rights reserved
Printed in the United States of America
First Edition

For information about permission to reproduce selections from this book, write to Permissions, W. W. Norton & Company, Inc., 500 Fifth Avenue, New York, NY 10110

For information about special discounts for bulk purchases, please contact W. W. Norton Special Sales at specialsales@wwnorton.com or 800-233-4830

Manufacturing by Versa Press
Book design by Hana Anouk Nakamura
Production manager: Delaney Adams

Library of Congress Cataloging-in-Publication Data is available.

ISBN 978-1-32405-353-8

W. W. Norton & Company, Inc., 500 Fifth Avenue, New York, NY 10110
www.wwnorton.com

W. W. Norton & Company Ltd., 15 Carlisle Street, London W1D 3BS

1 2 3 4 5 6 7 8 9 0

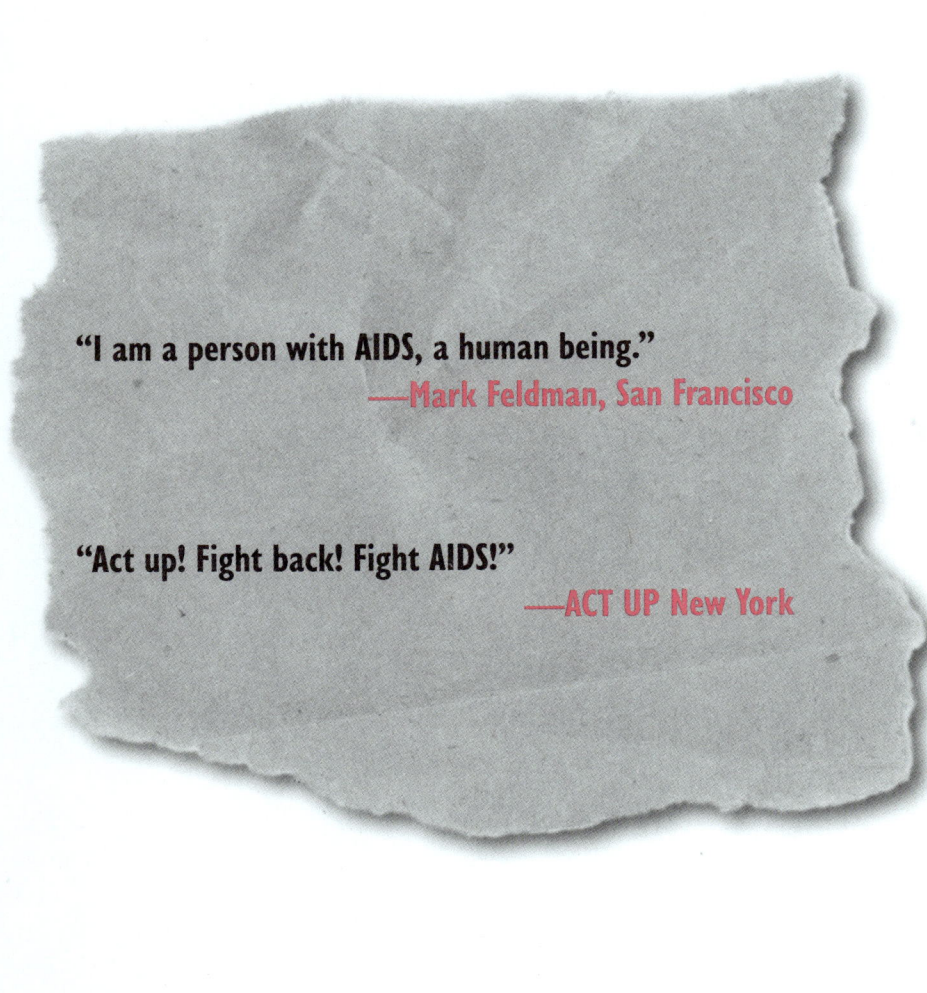

"I am a person with AIDS, a human being."
—Mark Feldman, San Francisco

"Act up! Fight back! Fight AIDS!"
—ACT UP New York

CONTENTS

Basic Facts 1

Part One: Before AIDS

1   Stonewall 7
2   Sexual Liberation 12
3   Do-It-Yourself Health Care 15

Part Two: The Fight Begins

4   A Chef, a Nurse, and a Teacher 23
5   Sharing the News 27
6   More Pneumonia, More Cancer 31
7   Raising Money 35

Part Three: Coming Out, Taking Care

8   Bobbi Hangs a Poster 41
9   Emotional Support 46
10   Traci Gets a Buddy 50
11   From GRID to AIDS 56
12   Calling for Condoms 59
13   The Missing White House 64

Part Four: From Care to Protest

14   Taking It to the Streets 71
15   People with AIDS 75
16   A Revolution on Ward 5B 79
17   Dying and Discovering 84
18   The Bathhouse Battles 90

Part Five: Turning Points

19	A Hollywood Heartthrob	97
20	A Midwestern Teen	102
21	Positive Change, Creative Protest	107
22	Corpses Everywhere	111
23	Blood Tests, Blood Sisters	115

Part Six: For Drugs, Against Silence

24	AZT Arrives	121
25	Buyers' Clubs	124
26	The Mob Screams	128
27	SILENCE = DEATH	134
28	ACT UP!	139

Part Seven: Comfort and Challenge

29	The AIDS Quilt	149
30	The Largest Protest	155
31	Ryan White Testifies	159

Part Eight: Act Up! Fight Back! Fight AIDS!

32	Seize Control of the FDA!	169
33	Dropping Prices, Exchanging Needles	174
34	Storm the NIH!	179
35	Wins and Losses	184

Part Nine: Congress and the Courts, Broadway and the White House

36	The Legacy of Ryan White	193
37	Women, Poor People, and Discrimination	198
38	Wearing Red Ribbons	205
39	Ashes for the White House	209
40	Victories Despite Death	214

Part Ten: From Bleakness to Breakthrough

41	One of the Bleakest Moments	221
42	Shock and Awe	227
43	Undetectable	233

Epilogue: An Unfinished Legacy 237
Acknowledgments 243
Notes 245
Image Credits.. 263
Index 265

A Note About the Art

Artists played a vital role during the AIDS epidemic. Their works, ranging from film and theater to music and dance, poetry and drawings, lamented the dead, honored the dying, and challenged the living. This book features some of the visual art that raised awareness about AIDS and beckoned everyday citizens to join the fight: posters and paintings, quilts and ribbons, and buttons and stickers. While some of these works were quiet, indirect, and unassuming, others were loud, confrontational, and full of fury. The most influential and striking include the pieces that introduce the ten parts of this book.

"FIGHT AIDS." A poster created by the activist organization ACT UP New York in the early 1990s.

BASIC FACTS

THE PATIENT WAS EXHAUSTED. HIS SEVERE DIARRHEA AND DRY COUGH MADE IT impossible to get a good night's sleep.

Making matters worse, the doctors in the gastroenterology clinic failed to appreciate just how sick he was. They even talked of sending him home.

Hearing that, the young man plopped down and pounded the floor, shocking the doctors and everyone else nearby. "I'm sick," he said. "I need to be in the hospital."

FIGHT AIDS

This outburst was an early and modest protest in the long fight against HIV and AIDS in the United States. Together with countless others, the patient's cry evolved into a powerful social movement that fought HIV and AIDS on multiple fronts.

The movement faced enormous obstacles, but in its early stages, nothing was more challenging than lack of basic knowledge about HIV and AIDS. To understand this point as it unfolds in the pages ahead, here are some of the facts currently provided by the US Centers for Disease Control and Prevention.

What is HIV?

HIV (human immunodeficiency virus) is a virus that attacks the body's immune system.

There is currently no effective cure.

With proper medical care, HIV can be controlled. People with HIV who get effective HIV treatment can live long, healthy lives and protect their partners.

What is AIDS?

If HIV is not treated, it can lead to AIDS (acquired immune deficiency syndrome).

AIDS is the last, and most severe, stage of HIV infection.

People with AIDS have a large amount of HIV in their blood and can easily transmit the virus to others.

They also have badly damaged immune systems that can result in deadly infections and other serious illnesses.

Without HIV treatment, people with AIDS typically survive about three years.

How is HIV passed from one person to another?

By semen and blood.

Sexual contact, sharing needles to inject drugs, giving birth, and breastfeeding are ways that HIV passes from one person to another.

HIV is not transmitted by air, water, saliva, sweat, or tears.

Nor by closed-mouth kissing, or sharing toilets, food, or drinks.

What are some ways for people to protect themselves from HIV?

If people engage in vaginal or anal sex, they can use condoms.

If people inject drugs, they can use clean needles.

PrEP (pre-exposure prophylaxis) is a medicine that reduces someone's chances of getting HIV from sex or drug injections.

PEP (post-exposure prophylaxis) is a medicine that can prevent HIV after possible exposure to it.

Where did HIV in humans come from?
A type of chimpanzee in Central Africa.

Studies show that HIV may have jumped from chimpanzees to humans as far back as the late 1800s.

It was probably passed to humans when they hunted these chimpanzees for meat and came in contact with their infected blood.

None of this information was known in 1981, when the organized fight against AIDS started to take shape. This is the story of the people who battled the AIDS epidemic between 1981, when HIV was not yet discovered, and 1996, when a combination of drugs made HIV undetectable in a person's blood. Their desperate fight for life remains one of the most significant—and untaught—events in US history.

PART ONE
BEFORE AIDS

STONEWALL '69

RIOT

AIDS CRISIS '89

"RIOT." A painting created by a group of artist-activists called Gran Fury in 1988 and turned into stickers and flyers connecting the AIDS epidemic and the 1969 Stonewall protests (above).

1

STONEWALL

MARK SEGAL WANTED TO BE WITH LOTS OF OTHER GAY MEN, SO IN JUNE 1969, JUST after graduating from high school, he left Philadelphia and moved to New York City.

One night, while strolling through Greenwich Village, he saw a bar that intrigued him—the Stonewall Inn. Not knowing what to expect, he dug into his pocket and paid the cover charge.

The place was grungy. The walls were black, the floor was sticky, and the air reeked of cigarette smoke and cologne.

But look at this! Two dance floors were filled with gay men, lesbian women, crossdressing folks, and people of all colors. Some of the same-sex couples were even kissing.

Segal was smitten.

On Friday, June 27, 1969, he was back for more fun. But then the lights flickered—the dreaded signal that the police were about to raid the place.

Inspector Seymour Pine pounded on the front door. "Police! We're taking the place!"

Raiding gay bars was a common practice for the New York Police Department (NYPD). Although it was legal for bars to serve gay men and lesbian women, the police often used other reasons to justify their raids. Tonight's reason was that the Stonewall did not have a proper liquor license.

Storming inside, the officers barked out orders. *Line up! And get your IDs out!*

While Segal and his friends searched for their IDs, several officers began arresting the bar's employees and gender-nonconforming patrons—the employees for serving liquor illegally, and the crossdressing folks for breaking a law prohibiting "unnatural attire."

The police checked Segal's ID, determined he was of legal drinking age (eighteen at the time), and pointed him toward the exit. Relieved, Segal stepped outside, but rather than leaving the scene, he and others stuck around, spouting off about the raid to one another and passersby. Before long, the crowd swelled with hundreds of unhappy LGBTQ people.

The parade of arrests began when officers escorted the bar's employees to waiting police cars and a paddy wagon. Then came the underage drinkers and the crossdressing folks. Some played up their arrest, blowing kisses at the crowd and strutting their way toward the cars.

The crowd clapped for their defiant comrades, but when they saw officers being rough with "the queens," or the crossdressing men, the cheers turned to angry jeers.

Inside the bar, a lesbian woman in pants fought back when an officer rough-handled her. After he whacked her on the head with his nightstick, his colleagues swarmed and slapped handcuffs on her. But she continued to resist.

Eventually, officers dragged her out of the bar and pushed her into a police car. She escaped—twice. As an officer shoved her back inside the car, she pleaded with the gawking crowd. "Why don't you guys do something?"

They did—they exploded.

"Pigs!" they shouted. Gay and gender-nonconforming street teens whipped coins at the officers' heads, and other enraged protesters quickly turned violent, hurling bottles and bricks and cans and cobblestones. One group surrounded the police cars and the paddy wagon, banging on them and rocking them back and forth.

"I wanted to kill those cops for all the anger I had in me," John O'Brien said later.

Protestors and police outside New York's Stonewall Inn, June 28, 1969.

Like countless others, O'Brien had years of pent-up anger over police harassment. And police brutality. And all the bigotry and hatred that LGBTQ folks faced simply because they were LGBTQ.

It was everywhere. Preachers denounced them as sexual perverts destined for hell. Psychiatrists labeled them as sociopathic, fit to be hospitalized and given shock therapy. Politicians saw them as criminals, a threat to the nation's children, the potential downfall of society, and deserving of imprisonment.

And countless others followed suit. Real estate managers evicted them—legally. Employers fired them—legally. Schools expelled them—legally. Friends deserted them. Families disowned them. And police officers beat the hell out of them.

"We all had a collective feeling like we'd had enough of this kind of shit," protester Michael Fader recalled. "It was like a last straw.... There was something in the air, freedom a long time overdue, and we're going to fight for it."

The furious fight ended about four in the morning. No one had died, but the NYPD had shown up in full riot gear, bloodying bodies and cracking skulls. Nearby streets were littered with trash, glass shards, and broken bricks.

For Segal and other LGBTQ folks, the war scene wasn't evidence of defeat. It was an inspiring symbol of power—their ability to fight back.

"Gay power!" they shouted the following night. Another full-scale protest, marked by bricks, rocks, Molotov cocktails, and tear gas, lasted until about 3:00 a.m.

Craig Rodwell—the owner of the first gay bookstore on the East

Coast—soon wrote and hung a flyer explaining the significance of the two protests.

> The nights of Friday, June 27, 1969, and Saturday, June 28, will go down in history as the first time that thousands of Homosexual men and women went out into the streets to protest the intolerable situation which has existed in New York City for many years.

That was a modest claim. The Stonewall uprising also marked the first time in world history that thousands of LGBTQ people engaged in street protests about LGBTQ-related injustices.

More fighting occurred three nights later, but it lasted only an hour or so. Although the protests were now over, the spirit of Stonewall—defiant, confrontational, and fierce—did not disappear into the night. It deeply embedded itself in the lives of those who took part and those inspired by the uprising. And in the days and decades to come, the Stonewall spirit would arise wherever and whenever the LGBTQ community faced deadly threats.

2

SEXUAL LIBERATION

PERRY BRASS NEVER LIKED THE STONEWALL INN. HE CALLED IT "A TOILET," A DOWN and dirty place run by a bunch of thuggish characters. But the twenty-four-year-old gay man was thrilled about the protests and the emerging militancy among his friends and acquaintances.

In the wake of the protests, LGBTQ militants started new organizations, including the Gay Liberation Front (GLF), whose fundamental belief was that "sexual liberation for all people cannot come unless existing social institutions are abolished." According to GLF, sexual liberation required bursting out of the closet, declaring your sexual orientation, and smashing laws, customs, and institutions that oppressed LGBTQ people. *Smash the church! Smash the state! Smash the medical establishment! And, above all else, smash traditional sexual morality!*

Brass attended GLF's consciousness-raising groups, where members talked about civil rights, the Vietnam War, and patriarchy, among other hot-button topics. He also loved going to GLF-sponsored dances, with their acid rock and strobe lights, their cheap beer and circle dancing, and their gender fluidity and sexual freedom. Like others in GLF, Brass was committed to the fullest expression of sexual liberation.

SEXUAL LIBERATION

Gay Liberation Front march in New York's Times Square, fall 1969.

For sex, Brass preferred Club Baths on New York's First Avenue. On a typical visit, he would arrive at the club around 11:00 p.m. and leave just as the sun was rising.

In between, he would hang out with friends or strangers outside the "orgy room," looking for just the right man to walk by, preferably twenty-something, clean, and well-groomed. If someone caught his attention, Brass would follow him into the orgy room, and if he showed interest in return, they would have sex. By the break of dawn, Brass would have had sex with three or four different men.

The whole experience, he said, was "like having a glorious party" that celebrated gay identity, gay community, and gay liberation. However much he enjoyed it, though, Brass also recognized that the glorious party could also leave one with a hangover. Or a disease.

Brass knew all about the various symptoms of gonorrhea—pus on the penis, an itchy anus, a swollen testicle, a sore throat—and in the spring of 1971, he was pretty sure he had it. He also had a pretty good idea that he had contracted it from his friend Burt.

The two young men decided to seek treatment at St. Mark's Clinic, a free public health clinic in the heart of Greenwich Village. Burt went with one doctor, Brass with another, and both explained they were seeking treatment for gonorrhea.

The doctors were far from surprised. Gonorrhea and other sexually transmitted diseases (STDs) were spreading like wildfire among gay men, largely because they were coming out in record numbers and hooking up in all the new baths and bars and nightclubs and gyms.

After examining Brass and Burt, the doctors met in the hallway and discussed their respective patients, including their practice of anal intercourse. Referring to either Brass or Burt, one of the doctors said, "Yes, I guess he was playing the 'male role.'"

Brass was stunned when he overheard the doctor's suggestion that he and Burt had assumed the traditional roles of heterosexual intercourse—male on top, female on bottom. Irritated and angry, he shared the comment with Burt when both were back in the waiting room. "Hell," Burt snorted, "you should have said that we weren't playing any roles. We were *fucking*."

For Brass and Burt, gay liberation meant freedom from traditional gender roles as they related to sexual behavior. It meant moving from top to bottom or bottom to top, or sideways or upside down, and not assigning gender roles to any position. It meant being themselves, whoever they were in the moment, and having sex in whatever way they wished.

The doctor's comments so disgusted the two young men that they stormed out the door, longing for a place where medical staff wouldn't try to stuff patients into small and suffocating boxes built by straight society. A place where gay men could receive health care without facing bigotry. A place where they could be safe.

3

DO-IT-YOURSELF HEALTH CARE

ALICE BLOCH, A NEWLY OUT LESBIAN WOMAN, AND LENNY EBREO, A NEWLY OUT GAY man, toured the drab basement of 247 West Eleventh Street in Greenwich Village. Cobwebs draped from the ceiling and bugs darted this way and that, but the rock-bottom price was perfect.

The two friends signed a lease, rounded up a few lamps and chairs, and converted the basement into Liberation House, a community center for LGBTQ people. The center soon housed a helpline for the LGBTQ community and hosted consciousness-raising groups.

Ebreo started a group on gay men's health, and Perry Brass signed up for it. The first two discussions focused on all the earthy details of the penis and the anus. *Oh, my god!* Brass thought, shocked and excited by the chance to speak so openly about the male body.

A few weeks later, Ebreo suggested that the group sponsor a public forum on STDs. To their surprise, about 125 men showed up. The speaker, an openly gay doctor, warned that untreated STDs could lead to severe problems like impotence, blindness, and death. He also offered an important piece of advice: *Wear condoms for protection!*

Audience members were surprised, even puzzled, because they had thought that condoms were only for birth control. They were also wary because condoms seemed so out of place in the era of sexual liberation. *Cover our penises in latex? We want to be free, not restricted!*

FIGHT AIDS

Pleased with the forum, Ebreo pitched another idea to Brass and a mutual friend, Marc Rabinowitz. *Let's start a gay men's health clinic!*

The three friends knew nothing about starting and running a clinic, but they were also painfully aware of the desperate need for a place where gay men would be treated with respect and dignity. *Okay—let's do it!*

To figure out what to do, they read *Our Bodies, Ourselves*, a groundbreaking book by a group of Boston feminists who urged women to assume responsibility for their own health care. Inspired by the book, as well as the wider women's health care movement, the friends decided to start an STD clinic that would be run *by* gay men and *for* gay men.

Their initial plan was simple: Be sensitive and empathetic, collect blood samples and cultures, and take them to a licensed health care site that would test them for STDs.

Executing the plan was a bit more complicated. Ebreo knew a bit about drawing blood—he had taken a Red Cross course—but Brass and Rabinowitz had no experience at all. So Ebreo shared his basic knowledge, and the trio practiced on one another until they felt capable and comfortable.

The group also learned how to take penile and anal cultures: Clean the opening, insert a cotton swab, gently rotate, and remove. Again, the friends practiced on one another until they felt confident enough.

Satisfied with their progress, the trio cleared a space at Liberation House and filled it with chairs, examination tables, and privacy screens. Someone persuaded the nearby Chelsea public health clinic to provide medical supplies—swabs, petri dishes, needles, vials, and bandages.

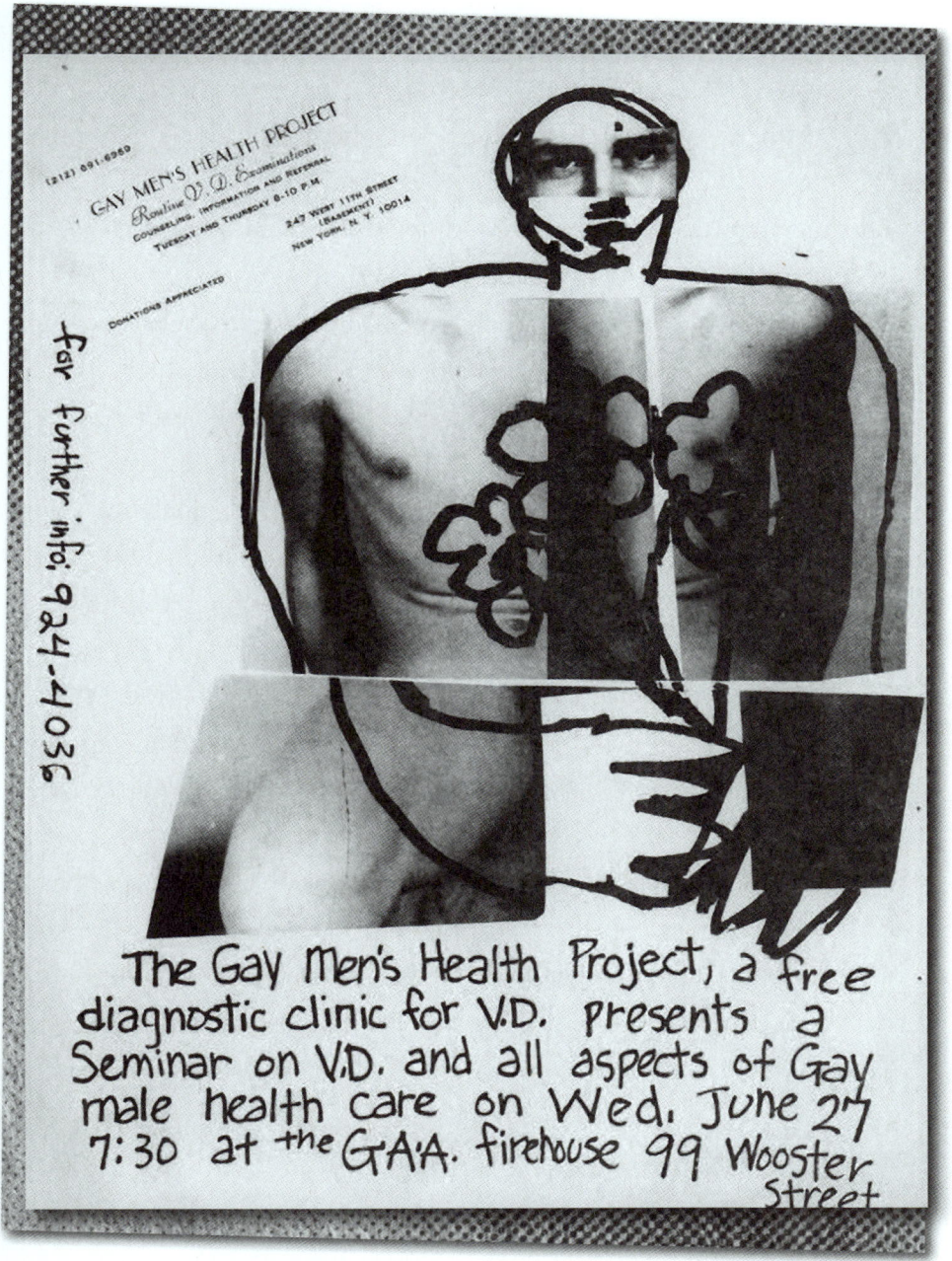

Flyer advertising the Gay Men's Health Project clinic, 1972.

The Gay Men's Health Project opened on a Tuesday night in the fall of 1972. As the trio of friends waited for their first clients, they feared that the New York City Department of Health would blast through the door and shut them down. After all, no one there had an official license to practice health care.

They also wondered whether anyone would show up, but those fears were soon calmed. "A few men nervously came in, then others," Brass recalled. "Then I walked out of the basement and saw that there was a line literally halfway down the block. I almost cried."

Not long after the successful opening, Dr. Dan William, a gay medical intern, joined the team of three. His presence made it easier for the Department of Health to support the start-up clinic as an official collection site for STD testing.

The clinic was soon open three nights a week, attracting professionally trained volunteers and serving hundreds of gay men. "We got men of every race, class, background, and political stripe," Brass recalled.

The clinic also went mobile, visiting gay bathhouses and other areas known for anonymous sex, including the Ramble, a secluded spot in Central Park, and a place known as "the Trucks," a parking area near the waterfront. As gay men had sex all around them, Brass and his team encouraged them to take care of their health—and to take a free condom.

Word about the Gay Men's Health Project spread fast, and other gay men's health clinics sprouted up across the country, from Boston to Chicago to Los Angeles. By the end of the 1970s, more than two dozen gay health clinics in the United States were testing and treating gay men with STDs.

By this point, Brass had left the Gay Men's Health Project. He had experienced burnout and longed to return to his creative endeavors, especially writing. But he stayed attuned to health care issues, and in the late 1970s, when he was working in a publishing house, he noticed something odd. His friends were developing strange illnesses that were highly unusual for otherwise healthy gay men. *This is really freaky,* Brass thought.

Dan William saw the same oddities at the clinic, and not only were the illnesses growing in number—they were also life-threatening.

PART TWO
THE FIGHT BEGINS

WE'RE FIRED UP

"WE'RE FIRED UP." Protest poster created by ACT UP, early 1990s.

4

A CHEF, A NURSE, AND A TEACHER

THE CHEF RUSHED TO THE NEAREST BATHROOM.

His diarrhea, with its burning pain, was virtually unbearable, and he barely made it to the toilet before it gushed out. The bowl was filled with blood.

This bout was unlike others. It was severe, it was relentless, and it was scary. Whatever this was, he had to fight it. Or it would kill him.

FIGHT AIDS

In July 1980, Dr. Donna Mildvan, an infectious disease specialist at New York's Beth Israel Hospital, not far from the Gay Men's Health Project, was puzzled by the patient in front of her—a thirty-three-year-old gay man from Germany who had recently been a chef in Haiti.

Mildvan noted that the chef's white blood cell count was low, which suggested that his immune system was compromised, or weakened. She also suspected that he might have an inflammatory bowel disease.

The chef's body responded well enough to standard medications, and he was soon discharged from the hospital. But three weeks later, he was back. The painful diarrhea had returned, and he was rapidly losing weight.

Mildvan and her team conducted more tests, and the chef's condition continued to worsen. For the next several months, he was in and out of the hospital, struggling to fight whatever was wreaking havoc on his body. His weight plummeted. His lymph nodes enlarged. His rectal area developed sores. He even lost vision in an eye.

What are we missing? Mildvan wondered. She suspected some sort of virus, and subsequent tests revealed the presence of genital herpes and cytomegalovirus (CMV), a herpes virus that can harm a patient's eyes and organs. The results were helpful, but Mildvan was still perplexed, even dumbfounded, because neither virus typically resulted in the horrific symptoms suffered by the chef.

The stubborn symptoms were proving untreatable. The chef soon went totally blind. Worse, his brain started to shrink. He became unable to speak. Unable to move his limbs. Unable to control his bowels. Wasting away, his skeletal body curled into itself.

In December 1980, just six months after entering the hospital, he died.

Mildvan and her team soon encountered another mysterious case. A gay nurse—whose energy had been sapped by fever, coughing, chest pains, and chills—had tested positive for pneumocystis pneumonia (PCP).

Patients with PCP were typically folks with weakened immune systems, like elderly patients or those with serious cancer, but the nurse wasn't typical by any stretch of the imagination. He wasn't elderly, and he wasn't a cancer patient.

Just like the chef, though, the nurse had a severe case of enlarged lymph nodes, revealing that his immune system was badly compromised and that he was trying to fight a nasty infection tearing through his body.

Ten days after entering the hospital, the nurse died.

Again, Mildvan and her team were shocked. When postmortem tests showed that the nurse and the chef both had a virus—cytomegalovirus—Mildvan was convinced: *This is a new disease, and it's attacking gay men.*

FIGHT AIDS

In January 1981, Mildvan had lunch with her friend and colleague, Dan William, the medical director at the Gay Men's Health Project. Mildvan told him about the two recent deaths and shared her suspicion that a new disease was emerging among gay men, and that it had something to do with a virus that was weakening immune systems and resulting in strange infections like pneumocystis pneumonia.

William listened intently. Then he shared his own shocking news: He had recently seen lots of gay patients with enlarged lymph nodes, as well as unusual cases of shingles, a rash with painful blisters, which typically appeared in people with compromised immune systems. But there was no obvious reason why the immune systems of otherwise healthy gay men were so weak.

There was more. "Donna, you're not going to believe what I have to tell you," Dan said. "Three patients of mine have Kaposi's sarcoma. Gay men. For no reason."

Kaposi's sarcoma?

Both doctors knew that Kaposi's sarcoma (KS) was a rare disease that caused cancerous tumors to appear on the skin or in the gastrointestinal tract. On the skin, the tumors looked like red, purple, or brown lesions, or spots. In the gastrointestinal tract, the lesions appeared everywhere from the mouth to the anus. They were painful, they caused bleeding, and they could even spread to the lungs.

But KS patients were typically older men of Mediterranean, Middle Eastern, and Eastern European descent. Dan's patients did *not* fit the profile.

Could this be more evidence of a new disease attacking gay men?

Meanwhile, Dr. Alvin Friedman-Kien, a dermatologist and microbiologist at New York University's medical center, was treating two patients, both young gay men, with Kaposi's sarcoma.

When he mentioned the oddity to his colleagues, Dr. Linda Laubenstein said that she, too, had recently diagnosed KS in gay men, including Rick Wellikoff, a gay physical education teacher who had already died.

Stunned by Laubenstein's report, Friedman-Kien called colleagues in other places to see whether they had any similar cases. Before long, he learned of more than a dozen. All were gay men in the New York area, all had an aggressive form of KS, and all were dying.

On April 22, 1981, Friedman-Kien spoke with his friend Marcus Conant, a gay dermatologist who lived and worked in San Francisco. Sure enough, one day later, Conant confirmed that KS was in the San Francisco area.

The outbreak had begun.

5

SHARING THE NEWS

DR. LARRY MASS DIDN'T RECOGNIZE THE NAME ON THE MESSAGE, BUT HE PICKED UP the phone and dialed the number.

"My doctor is Larry Downs," a young man explained. "Maybe I shouldn't be telling you this. Anyway, I overheard Larry say that there are four, maybe five, gay men in New York City intensive care units. They've all got some kind of weird pneumonia or something. I think he said two of them are dead."

Mass wrote articles for a gay newspaper, the *New York Native*. He wasn't sure what to make of the call, but he knew that it was a tip worth pursuing.

Later that same day, he spoke with Dr. Joyce Wallace, who was affiliated with St. Vincent's Hospital. Wallace was never easy to understand, but this time her comments were even more disjointed and cryptic than usual.

"They told me not to say anything," she said.

"They?" Mass wondered. "Who are they?"

Wallace sounded uncomfortable and upset. "There are some gay men in intensive care units, and they're very sick with pneumonia," she added. "But I'm not supposed to tell anyone."

The call lasted only a minute before Wallace hung up rather abruptly.

Crazy Joyce, Mass thought.

Mass had met Wallace a year earlier, at a get-together of community physicians in Greenwich Village. He was the codirector of a methadone maintenance clinic, and she had a private practice where she treated drug users, LGBTQ folks, and streetwalking sex workers. The two doctors took a liking to each other and quickly became friends.

About once a month, they also met with a small group of colleagues—including Dan William of the Gay Men's Health Project—to share news about local health concerns and trends. Sometimes the topics landed in the articles that Mass penned for the *New York Native*.

But what could he write about these two calls? Gay men, pneumonia, intensive care units—the information was far too scant for an article.

So Mass phoned the New York City Department of Health and Mental Hygiene, where he was put in touch with Dr. Steven Phillips, who monitored disease patterns in the city. Without revealing his sources, Mass asked Phillips whether he knew anything about rumors of gay men with pneumonia in local intensive care units.

"Well," Phillips replied, "there were, in fact, some cases, and there was just not enough information about them to draw any conclusions."

Maybe Joyce Wallace wasn't so crazy after all.

Mass looked at the blank sheet of paper. He did not have a lot to write about, but he believed that the gay community had a right to know the little information that was available.

"Last week," he typed, "there were rumors that an exotic new disease had hit the gay community in New York. Here are the facts."

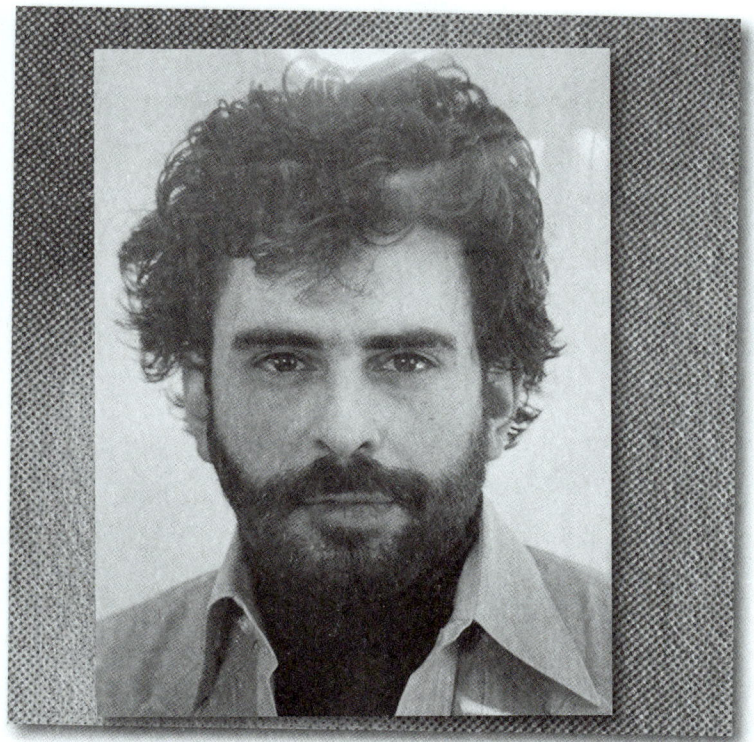

Dr. Larry Mass.

Mass strove to be clear and concise—and careful. While he wanted to sound the alarm about the infection, he did not want to sound it too loudly. His goals were to educate readers about the infection and help them understand that the facts did not warrant panic.

"Each year," he typed on, "approximately 12 to 24 cases of... [pneumocystis pneumonia] are reported in the New York City area."

This type of pneumonia was nothing out of the ordinary, Mass explained, and most people have an immune system that can fight and kill it. Individuals with weakened immune systems, however, were susceptible to the infection.

But there *was* something unusual in recent cases, Mass added. The infection appeared in individuals whose immune system was not "obviously compromised." They weren't like elderly cancer patients with weakened systems, and this suggested the possibility of a new and infectious disease.

And yes, gay men were among the reported cases. "But of the eleven cases this year that have been tentatively identified as community acquired, only five or six have been gay." One had already died.

Pulling the paper from his typewriter, Mass felt satisfied enough with the article. It stuck to the known facts, and it raised awareness of pneumocystis pneumonia. It also avoided any suggestion that gay men were the source of a deadly disease that might spread to the public. Gay and Jewish, Mass was aware of how gay men could be scapegoated, and he feared the possibility that rumors of a gay disease would result in a new round of targeting.

Chuck Ortleb gave the article a careful read. As a skilled editor, he probably noted that it had only one source, that its facts were few, and that it left readers with a troubling question: *Why were otherwise healthy gay men coming down with pneumocystis pneumonia?*

But Ortleb, like Mass, quickly grasped the story's significance. The possibility that a new disease was attacking gay men was downright scary.

And newsworthy.

On May 18, 1981, Mass's article appeared below the fold on the second page of the *New York Native*. It was the first published article about a disease that would shake the entire world.

6

MORE PNEUMONIA, MORE CANCER

ON JUNE 5, 1981, THE *MORBIDITY AND MORTALITY WEEKLY REPORT*, A NEWSLETTER published by the Centers for Disease Control (CDC), reported on a cluster of five gay men, in Los Angeles, with pneumocystis pneumonia.

Three days later, the CDC—the federal agency that seeks to protect the country from health threats—created a task force to track and monitor pneumocystis pneumonia, Kaposi's sarcoma, and other "opportunistic infections," or infections that often occur in people with weakened immune systems.

FIGHT AIDS

A month later, on July 3, Eric Marcus took a bite of his Cheerios, topped with sliced bananas, in his small apartment at 44th Street and Ninth Avenue in New York City. He and his college roommate, Doug Aucoin, had moved there after graduating from Vassar College.

The apartment was quiet—Aucoin was still in bed—and Marcus scanned the first page of the *New York Times*. A photo of Björn Borg, the handsome tennis player from Sweden, graced the page.

A headline on page 20 also caught Marcus's attention—"Rare Cancer

Seen in 41 Homosexuals." The subtitle sounded just as ominous—"Outbreak Occurs Among Men in New York and California—8 Died Inside 2 Years."

A cancer called Kaposi's sarcoma, Marcus read, "appears in one or more violet-colored spots anywhere on the body" and "often causes swollen lymph glands, and then kills by spreading throughout the body."

Intrigued, Marcus read on. "The reporting doctors said that most cases had involved homosexual men who have had multiple and frequent sexual encounters with different partners, as many as 10 sexual encounters each night up to four times a week."

What did these guys expect? Marcus thought. Sure, he'd had twenty or so sexual partners, but that was over several years. Only gay men who lived in the baths could rack up those kinds of numbers, and Marcus was most definitely not one of those guys.

By the time he finished his

RARE CANCER SEEN IN 41 HOMOSEXUALS

Outbreak Occurs Among Men in New York and California —8 Died Inside 2 Years

By LAWRENCE K. ALTMAN

Doctors in New York and California have diagnosed among homosexual men 41 cases of a rare and often rapidly fatal form of cancer. Eight of the victims died less than 24 months after the diagnosis was made.

The cause of the outbreak is unknown, and there is as yet no evidence of contagion. But the doctors who have made the diagnoses, mostly in New York City and the San Francisco Bay area, are alerting other physicians who treat large numbers of homosexual men to the problem in an effort to help identify more cases and to reduce the delay in offering chemotherapy treatment.

The sudden appearance of the cancer, called Kaposi's Sarcoma, has prompted a medical investigation that experts say could have as much scientific as public health importance because of what it may teach about determining the causes of more common types of cancer.

First Appears in Spots

Doctors have been taught in the past that the cancer usually appeared first in spots on the legs and that the disease took a slow course of up to 10 years. But these recent cases have shown that it appears in one or more violet-colored spots anywhere on the body. The spots generally do not itch or cause other symptoms, often can be mistaken for bruises, sometimes appear as lumps and can turn brown after a period of time. The cancer often causes swollen lymph glands, and then kills by spreading throughout the body.

News item in the *New York Times*, July 3, 1981—one of the first mainstream media reports drawing attention to the growing epidemic.

breakfast, Marcus had decided that the news about Kaposi's sarcoma had little relation to his own gay life. He did not check himself for spots.

Fresh out of college, David France thought the *Times* article "seemed like a new slander on the gay community."

France was all too familiar with the slanderous treatment of LGBTQ people in the decade following the Stonewall riots. Because LGBTQ activists had pressed for equal treatment under law, forced psychiatrists to remove homosexuality from their list of mental disorders, and protested for antidiscrimination laws and the overturning of sodomy laws, a virulent backlash had erupted across the country. Politicians had stirred up voters, and preachers had roused the faithful, decrying "the gay agenda" threatening the American way of life.

Reading the *Times* with all this in mind, France thought the article "seemed like just another lie, a call to more hatred, a fiercer backlash."

Philip Gefter, a picture editor at *Forbes* magazine, was lounging around the pool of his Fire Island house when he read the article. *What the fuck?* he thought.

Gefter was pissed. Like thousands of gay New Yorkers, he had reveled in "the Gay Decade" of the 1970s. He had dived headfirst into gay politics and the gay bars and clubs where having sex was like shaking hands. Gay had become chic, and Gefter loved it.

We're lepers again, he thought, looking at the sparkling pool. *We're going to be ostracized again.*

FIGHT AIDS!

In Greenwich Village, the article scared the hell out of writer Larry Kramer, and he began to imagine that he too might be infected. Panicked, he made an appointment with Dr. Alvin Friedman-Kien at the NYU Medical Center.

On July 29, 1981, after examining him from head to toe, Friedman-Kien delivered his diagnosis—*Nothing*. But the doctor assured Kramer that his fears were well-grounded. "We're only seeing the tip of the iceberg," he said. "We don't know what it is. It would appear to be a virus, but we don't have any concrete evidence."

The doctor knew of Kramer's influence in the gay community and urged him to help spread the word. He also expressed his frustration with a lack of research funds, and asked whether Kramer might help raise some money. "I don't think anybody is going to give a damn, and it's really up to you guys to do something," he said.

You guys—gay men.

7

RAISING MONEY

WHILE LARRY KRAMER PLANNED A FUNDRAISING CAMPAIGN, LARRY MASS RESEARCHED Kaposi's sarcoma and used his next article—the first feature article on the new disease—to answer a series of questions about possible reasons for the link between gay men and the new disease.

Is there something about our genes that make us susceptible to KS?

No, Mass said. The susceptibility "can't be overridingly genetic because homosexuality itself has never been convincingly demonstrated to be so." Because there was no so-called gay gene, it was doubtful that gay men were genetically predisposed to KS.

What about poppers, the drugs we use to enhance sex? Or what about sexual lubricants? Could they be related to KS?

Probably not, Mass wrote, because not all KS patients had used poppers or the same lubricants.

What about anal insertions?

That's a bit more complicated. In fact, "cuts and abrasions" in the rectal lining "could predispose the receptor to the systemic spread" of intestinal infections.

So what can we do to protect ourselves?

"At this time," Mass wrote, "many feel that sexual frequency with a multiplicity of partners—what some would call promiscuity—is the single overriding risk factor for developing infectious diseases." So, to reduce risk, cut back on sex and the number of partners.

Mass did not mention using condoms.

FIGHT AIDS

On August 11, 1981, about seventy gay men packed into Larry Kramer's apartment, sipping wine, chatting about the new disease, and checking out the financial pledge cards distributed by a man with KS.

Then, Friedman-Kien claimed a spot in the middle of the room. Andy Humm—who led the gay and lesbian campaign for a citywide antidiscrimination law—noticed that the room grew quiet. "You could have heard a pin drop," he recalled.

Friedman-Kien covered virtually the same material found in Larry Mass's article, but with an important difference: This was a personal testimony. The doctor had seen the KS lesions. He had treated KS patients. He had watched them die.

Although he couldn't be certain the disease was "communicable," Friedman-Kien said that it seemed related to "gay sexual activity." Looking around the room, Humm detected a sense of dread in the crowd's expressions and body language.

The doctor also cautioned the group, saying that until experts could determine the cause of the new disease, as well as its mode of transmission, it would be prudent for gay men to stop using drugs and engaging in anal intercourse, and to be more selective in choosing their partners.

He did not mention using condoms.

Finally, during a nervous question-and-answer session, Friedman-Kien emphasized that the numbers of those with the disease would only increase in the foreseeable future. There was no end in sight.

As the evening wound down, Kramer passed the hat. The anxious crowd gave $6,635 to support research into the mysterious disease.

FIGHT AIDS

A short while later, the *Native* published a fundraising appeal penned by Kramer. It was the first published call to fight the emerging disease.

"It's difficult to write this without sounding alarmist or too emotional or just plain scared," Kramer wrote. "If I had written this a month ago, I would have used the figure '40.' If I had written this last week, I would have needed '80.' Today I must tell you that 120 gay men in the United States—most of them here in New York—are suffering from an often-lethal form of cancer called Kaposi's sarcoma or from a virulent form of pneumonia that may be associated with it. More than thirty have died."

Kramer then asked for money to support not only research but also sick patients who did not have enough money for treatment. "This is our disease and we must take care of each other and ourselves," he wrote. "In the past we have often been a divided community; I hope we can all get together on this emergency, undivided, cohesively, and with all the numbers we in so many ways possess."

In California, a gay nurse would soon make a similar plea.

PART THREE
COMING OUT, TAKING CARE

MEN
USE CONDOMS
OR BEAT IT

Gran Fury

"USE CONDOMS." Poster created by the activist-artist group Gran Fury, 1988.

8

BOBBI HANGS A POSTER

BOBBI CAMPBELL, A TWENTY-NINE-YEAR-OLD REGISTERED NURSE FROM SAN Francisco, relished the moment as he hiked through Big Sur, with its towering redwoods, flowery meadows, and panoramic views of the ocean. A hint of fall was in the air.

A hike had been out of the question at the beginning of the year. A severe case of shingles—the viral infection that Dan William had seen in his New York City patients—had landed Campbell in the hospital. Then, several months later, he suffered from a low white blood cell count that left him feverish and weak.

He had found the illnesses odd, especially the shingles, which usually hit people fifty and older, but now, with those sick days behind him, he plowed ahead with his partner, Ron, walking by his side.

FIGHT AIDS

Back home in his apartment, Campbell noticed several strange spots on his feet. They looked like blood blisters, so he didn't give them a second thought, but three weeks later, they were still there.

Campbell was worried. He had followed news reports of Kaposi's sarcoma (KS) among gay men, and he had read about the skin lesions. *Could I have cancer?* he wondered.

He soon scheduled a visit with Dr. Marcus Conant, the gay dermatologist whom Friedman-Kien had called when checking on the rise of KS cases. Conant was now codirecting the country's first KS clinic, at the University of California, San Francisco.

Examining Campbell's spots, Conant gently rubbed his fingers over their surface. They looked like KS lesions, but to be certain he ordered a biopsy.

On October 8, 1981, Conant shared the news—it was KS.

"I was stricken," Campbell later said. "It was a horrible experience to hear that I had cancer, that I had this disease that was potentially fatal."

Depression struck hard and fast. Campbell dealt with it through self-destructive behavior, drinking too much and taking illegal drugs. He also erupted at his therapist, his doctor, and his friends. Within a two-week period, he and Ron broke up and reconciled, twice.

At the same time, Campbell was determined to survive, and he started to wear a button with the title of Gloria Gaynor's 1979 hit song—"I Will Survive."

Campbell did not keep his thoughts to himself. On December 10, 1981, he came out as a gay man with KS on the front page of the *San Francisco Sentinel*.

"I'm Bobbi Campbell, and I have 'gay cancer,'" he announced.

After recounting the ways that the diagnosis had wreaked havoc in his life, Campbell said that he was beginning to channel his anger constructively.

"Since I'm a professed Gay health nurse, I decided that one way for me to help myself deal with this crisis was to be functional," he wrote. "I wanted to find out what needs the KS and PCP patients had that a nurse could address.

"What I found was that the doctors were treating the KS patients beautifully from a medical perspective. However, the men did not know each other, and a support system had not yet been implemented."

Bobbi Campbell.

To fill the gap, Campbell had begun working with the Shanti Project, a peer counseling organization, to create "a support group for all cancer-stricken gay men."

Campbell announced that he would also continue raising awareness about KS by writing articles for the *Sentinel* and other publications. Calling himself the "Kaposi's Sarcoma Poster Boy," he would seek to secure funds for research, too.

FIGHT AIDS

In the immediate days ahead, the Poster Boy turned his attention to the gayest neighborhood in San Francisco—the Castro. That's where Ed Wolf saw it.

Wolf wanted to smoke pot with his friend, Michael, before they caught the double feature at the Castro Theater. But they didn't have any papers for rolling joints. So Wolf dashed down Castro Street toward Star Pharmacy.

Just as he was about to bolt through the door, he stopped in his tracks. The title of a handmade poster hanging in the window captured his attention—"GAY CANCER." Bobbi Campbell had made and hung the poster to raise awareness among the thousands of gay men who walked up and down Castro Street.

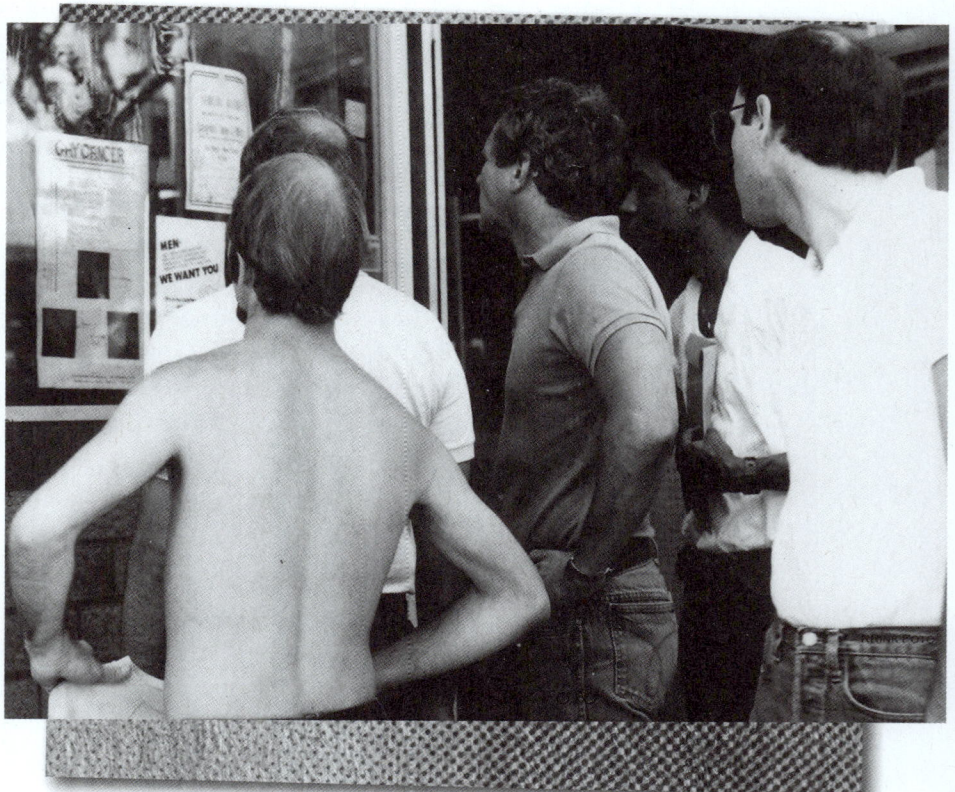

Men read a poster headlined "Gay Cancer" in a store window in San Francisco's Castro neighborhood, 1982.

Below the eye-popping title was a series of three graphic photos. Wolf was taken aback. The "big purple splotches" inside Campbell's mouth and all over his chest were so graphic, so awful.

No longer in a rush, Wolf went into the pharmacy and bought the papers. He and Michael got stoned, but the images of Campbell's spots wouldn't go away. Wolf thought of them throughout the entire double feature.

He and countless other gay men in the Castro neighborhood also began checking themselves, and their friends, for those ugly purple spots. Before long, many of them would begin finding them and would seek the support that Campbell had mentioned. They, too, were in emotional pain.

9

EMOTIONAL SUPPORT

ON A FALL EVENING IN 1981, BOBBI CAMPBELL ARRIVED AT JIM GEARY'S HOUSE ON Chattanooga Street, not far from the Castro district.

Geary, a gay counselor with the Shanti Project, warmly greeted Campbell at the front door and invited him to sit in the living room with two other gay men, John and Bill. The relaxed setting of a living room, with its plush couch and comfy chairs, was by design. Geary wanted the men to know that they were in a safe and supportive environment.

The men introduced themselves to one another and shared their diagnoses. John had Kaposi's sarcoma, and Bill suffered from lymphoma, cancer of the lymph system. While talking about his KS, Campbell took off his shoe and showed his foot lesions.

Loneliness was something they shared. The men said that their diagnoses made them feel all alone, even when they were with close friends who were sympathetic. Although appreciated, the sympathy couldn't quite reach the pain within.

When the men spoke of their families, the pain was palpable. In his soft voice, John shared that his two brothers disowned him when they learned he was gay.

The conversation was a bit lighter, though still intense, when

Campbell, the only medical expert in the group, shared his knowledge about treatment and its effects. The effects were already visible that night. John, a hair stylist, was losing his treasured hair because of chemotherapy, and Bill was thin and frail.

Campbell also spoke of feeling as if he was a guinea pig at the KS clinic. Medical staff members were taking countless biopsies of his lesions and testing them for insight into the disease. While he felt good about offering his body for study—that was a key part of his fight against the disease—the tests still left him feeling dehumanized, as if he was merely an object for poking and prodding.

For a moment, a heavy cloud descended on the conversation when the group discussed what might happen to them—the possibility of dying. *Will it hurt? How long will it take? Who will be there? Anyone?*

As they said their goodbyes, the men hugged one another. They weren't alone after all.

FIGHT AIDS

Campbell didn't want other gay men to stare into the abyss alone, so he regularly showed up at the KS clinic, introduced himself to other patients, and invited them to the Shanti group. He also encouraged the clinic's staff to share his phone number and address with new patients.

By March 1982, the Shanti group had grown to seven men. Campbell wrote about the group in his regular column for the *Sentinel*.

"While we have had additions, we've also had losses," he reported. "Bill died in his doctor's office on my 30th birthday. John died in the intensive care unit a month later. Other brothers, too sick to come to meetings, also have succumbed to their illness."

Campbell also described what the group usually discussed. "Topics for conversation come and go: experiences with doctors and hospitals, reactions of friends and family, sexual adaptations, hope for cure and fear of death, and even—should worse come to worse—the possibility of suicide."

But the group also did more than sit around and chat, Campbell reported. After the group finished sharing, a Shanti leader guided

Flyer calling for volunteers for a Shanti Project counseling group.

everyone in an exercise that included relaxation and visualization. The men lay on the floor, relaxed their bodies, and imagined their cancer cells dying and their immune systems strengthening. "It's been known to work," Campbell said.

At the end of the visualization, the men returned to their feet. "We form a tight circle and hug each other for several minutes—sometimes we cry. It's a high point of my week. These men know what I'm going through more than anyone else ever could."

It was do-it-yourself emotional support—by sick gay men, for sick gay men. For them, taking care of one another's emotional needs was one of the best ways to fight the disease, even if they died in the process.

FIGHT AIDS

As the group continued to grow, so did the fear surrounding the mysterious illness, partly because of unanswered questions about how it passed from one person to another. Could you catch it by touching someone sick? By standing next to them? By inhaling germs from their cough? By using the same toilet? By touching a shared handrail?

Group members shared stories about fearful roommates asking them to move out. And about health care providers refusing to touch them, and friends ignoring them, and employers firing them. Then there were the funeral directors who refused to handle the bodies of their deceased friends. The hair-raising stories ensured the need for ongoing emotional support.

Back in New York City, gay leaders were thinking about other ways to offer support.

10

TRACI GETS A BUDDY

WE NEED TO DO MORE! RAISE MORE MONEY FOR RESEARCH. EDUCATE THE PUBLIC. *Take care of people with the disease. And whatever else comes up.*

On the evening of January 4, 1982, six gay men in Larry Kramer's apartment resolved to create a nonprofit organization that would expand efforts to fight the new disease. "Gay men certainly do have a health crisis," one of the men lamented.

"Let's use that for our name, 'Gay Men's Health Crisis,'" Kramer said.

Larry Mass shifted in his seat, uncomfortable with the plan to identify the new disease so closely with the gay community. *What about blowback? Won't all gay men be labeled as health threats?*

The group understood Mass's objections, but they shook their heads. The name was perfect, they said, "because it showed that this was an attempt at community empowerment, that gay men were actually trying to help themselves."

They might not have realized it, but their do-it-yourself enthusiasm echoed the resolve expressed a decade earlier, when Perry Brass and his friends had boldly created the Gay Men's Health Project.

TRACI GETS A BUDDY

The phone in Rodger McFarlane's apartment wouldn't stop ringing. In May 1982, McFarlane used his own phone and answering machine to start a helpline, the first major service offered by the Gay Men's Health Crisis (GMHC).

"I had a hundred calls the first night from people in dire straits—very frightened," he said later. "And it was like that every night after that. It was terrifying, and no one would help."

Some of the callers cried out for immediate help. "I mean they were sitting in shit in Mount Sinai and NYU [hospitals]," McFarlane recalled. "And these are our friends and lovers, and you couldn't just let them lay in shit until you talked the nurses into cleaning them up."

Sometimes, McFarlane slammed the phone down and rushed to help callers in desperate need. He cleaned them. Wiped their tears. Held their hands. Promised them they wouldn't die alone. And then told the nursing staff to do their job.

If there was anything clear to McFarlane, it was that people were deathly afraid of catching the new disease, and that they were truly awful when dealing with those who had it. "We had a patient set on fire," he said. "This stuff was surreal. We had people literally beaten up with bats and thrown out of their apartments. You can't make this shit up."

With so many people in need, McFarlane quickly determined that GMHC needed to offer a lot more services than a hotline. What the organization urgently needed was a "buddy program" that would pair sick clients with GMHC volunteers who would visit them and take care of their basic needs. In September 1982, GMHC inaugurated a buddy program that would eventually help thousands of people.

The buddy trainer asked Hal Moskowitz, a 28-year-old nursing student, if he would be willing to volunteer for the Bronx. Moskowitz grasped the weight of the question. The New York borough was a tough place. It certainly wasn't as tolerant of gay people as Manhattan's Greenwich Village was, and some neighborhoods had high crime rates.

"Of course," Moskowitz replied. "I'll do whatever needs to be done."

Before long, GMHC gave him contact information for his first client. Excited, Moskowitz called to introduce himself and make plans for their first meeting. But the client didn't answer. He had already died.

GMHC soon called with another referral. Again, Moskowitz called to introduce himself.

Again, the client had already died. That happened three more times. "Oh, my God," Moskowitz said to himself. "I don't know if I can do this."

But he stayed the course and finally connected with his first client—a patient at the Bronx Lebanon Hospital. Walking into the hospital room, Moskowitz saw a very sick man in bed.

"Hi. I'm Hal, your buddy from the Gay Men's Health Crisis."

The patient smiled and introduced himself. He was a gay man in his twenties, an immigrant from the Dominican Republic, and he worked in retail.

"Is there anything I can do for you?" Moskowitz asked.

"Yes. Would you clean my apartment?"

The young man lived alone and hoped to return to a clean apartment as soon as he was well enough to leave the hospital.

"Of course," Moskowitz replied.

The young man never made it home.

Moskowitz still didn't quit, and he soon called his next referral from GMHC—Traci.

She spooked the hell out of him. The neighbors don't like strange people coming into the area, she said. And whatever you do, don't tell anybody where you're going. Or who you're seeing. Just don't talk to anyone.

Moskowitz kept his head down and his mouth shut. Breathing a sigh of relief, he made it to her front door without any problems. Inside, he saw festive lights, house plants galore, fun displays of pink and purple tchotchkes—and Traci. "She was Latinx, and she was beautiful!" Moskowitz recalled.

Volunteers in the cramped Gay Men's Health Crisis office, 1983.

Traci loved to chat, especially about her transgender identity. "I'm not a drag queen!" she announced. Although she had not had gender confirmation surgery, she did have breast implants—a gel injected by someone in the medical underground. She also had paid them to inject latex into her buttocks.

"I'm not a drug addict!" she added. But yes, she was a sex worker, and her two roommates were also sex workers. Traci strongly believed that her sex work was *not* the cause of her illness. She had gotten sick, she said, from injecting hormones to help with her transition.

Nothing about her sex work was too intimate to confide, even the sexual violence, but there was one subject that Traci wouldn't talk about—her family. They had disowned her years ago.

FIGHT AIDS

Traci and Moskowitz spent several weeks together. No matter how she was feeling, Traci always dressed to the nines, usually in a blouse, skirt, and a free-flowing robe. She always wore makeup, and if she wasn't sporting a perfectly coiffed wig, she pulled her hair back with a babushka scarf.

Traci had trouble walking, though, and sometimes she had uncontrollable diarrhea. Moskowitz offered to go to the grocery store for her, but she first had to school him in the art of picking ripe avocados and bananas.

The two spent hours on the couch, folding clothes and arranging them according to color. The two also talked about death. "I don't want to die," Traci said. "But nothing can be worse than what I've already been through."

Then, Traci was hospitalized with a severe case of pneumocystis pneumonia. Although she initially responded well to treatment, her breathing grew labored. Sitting beside her, Moskowitz was taken aback.

She didn't have any makeup on. There was no wig, no babushka scarf. No silky blouse. No flowing robes. No dramatic utterances.

Traci was having trouble swallowing, and a suction machine stood nearby. When Moskowitz finally left, he feared that if she started to choke, the medical staff would be too afraid to help her—too afraid of catching the disease.

The next day, Traci died. "The cause of death was choking," Moskowitz recalled, his voice drifting into sadness. "I can still smell her perfume. She always wore perfume."

Elsewhere, others were trying to avoid what Traci had just experienced, as the impact of the disease began to spread beyond the gay community. And in Atlanta, the Centers for Disease Control was struggling to keep up with all the different groups caught in the epidemic.

11

FROM GRID TO AIDS

BY THE END OF 1981, THE CENTERS FOR DISEASE CONTROL REPORTED THAT MORE than a dozen people had *both* Kaposi's sarcoma (KS) and opportunistic infections, including pneumocystis pneumonia. The co-occurrence suggested that KS and opportunistic infections were consequences of weakened immune systems—that "the epidemic was one of immunosuppression."

But what was damaging immune systems? Many researchers and medical doctors, including Dan William in New York and Marcus Conant in San Francisco, suspected a new virus. But the CDC did not have the scientific data required to prove their suspicions.

In early 1982, a new CDC report showed that forty of ninety patients in ten cities were linked by sexual contact with one gay man. The finding "strongly suggested that the new syndrome [KS and opportunistic infections] was caused by a sexually transmissible infectious agent."

What was the infectious agent? The CDC did not hazard a guess. Its lack of clarity was the reason that it used "syndrome" rather than "disease" to describe the medical mystery. Unlike diseases, syndromes are *related* health conditions, like KS and opportunistic infections, that do not have a definable cause. The CDC was a stickler for precision in language, even though most everyone else referred to the medical mystery as a new disease.

Another concern over language was brewing. Because sexually active gay men comprised the great majority of cases, some researchers were now using the term "GRID" (Gay-Related Immune Deficiency) to describe the new syndrome. The name gained further traction when the *New York Times* used it in a story on May 11, 1982. But other researchers balked at the term, noting that at least one heterosexual woman was among the reported cases. Two other developments would soon reveal the inexactness of "GRID."

On July 9, 1982, the CDC reported that KS and opportunistic infections had been diagnosed in forty Haitians who had migrated from Haiti to the United States.

A week later, the CDC stated that pneumocystis pneumonia had also turned up in people with hemophilia, a rare blood disorder that prevents blood from clotting. None of the cases had a history of gay sex.

By this point, doctors and researchers were also seeing KS and opportunistic infections in drug users, especially those who shared dirty needles when shooting heroin. So the CDC also stated that the patients with hemophilia had not shared needles with drug users with KS or opportunistic infections.

"GRID" collapsed. No longer could the syndrome be rightly described as a "homosexual disorder," or the "gay plague."

In September 1982, the CDC began to use the term "AIDS," or Acquired Immune Deficiency Syndrome. Still, the agency offered no information about what was causing the immune deficiency. The best that they could do was to identify risk factors.

So on September 24, the CDC stated that "AIDS cases may be separated into groups based on these risk factors: homosexual or bisexual males—75%, intravenous drug abusers with no history of male homosexual activity—13%, Haitians with neither a history of homosexuality nor a history of intravenous drug abuse—6%, persons with hemophilia A who were not Haitians, homosexuals, or intravenous drug abusers—0.3%, and persons in none of the other groups—5%."

The news grew worse, too. In December, the CDC revealed that an infant had developed an "unexplained cellular immunodeficiency and opportunistic infection." In January 1983, the agency also reported immunodeficiency among female sexual partners of men with AIDS.

The big question remained—*Why?*

In Greenwich Village, Dr. Joseph Sonnabend claimed to know the reason why AIDS was attacking gay men.

12

CALLING FOR CONDOMS

DR. JOSEPH SONNABEND—A VOLUNTEER FOR THE GAY MEN'S HEALTH PROJECT WHO also had a nearby private practice—hypothesized that weakened immunity in gay men resulted from repeated exposure to sperm containing viruses, particularly cytomegalovirus, and that it was possible to survive AIDS. But people had to "stop fucking around," he said. They had to give their bodies a break from fighting one STD after another. They had to start living a "healthy" lifestyle.

Sonnabend had two adoring patients who were committed to sharing his hypothesis as widely as possible: Richard Berkowitz and Michael Callen. Both had a personal history of prolific sex. Berkowitz was a former sex worker, and Callen claimed to have had sex with more than 3,000 men.

Both were also convinced that their "promiscuity," as they put it, had led to infections that broke down their immune system. Together, the two men shared their beliefs in an article for the *New York Native*—"We Know Who We Are: Two Gay Men Declare War on Promiscuity."

The article created a furor. Readers scoffed at the suggestion that weak immune systems resulted from a promiscuous lifestyle marked by repeated infections. Promiscuity wasn't the problem—exposure to a killer virus was the problem.

Readers also saw the "war on promiscuity" as a direct assault on the sexual liberation that LGBTQ folks had fought so hard to win. Callen and Berkowitz were dismissed as uneducated sexual Puritans, evangelists for traditional sexual morality.

But then Berkowitz had an epiphany.

Tom rang Berkowitz's doorbell. The former client had tried calling, but when he couldn't get a hold of Berkowitz, he decided to just show up. Reluctantly, Berkowitz invited him in and explained that he was no longer a sex worker. But, as Berkowitz recalled the visit, "Tom wanted sex and he wanted it now, and I wanted the $100."

Feeling rather desperate, Tom suggested that they engage in their regular roleplay—Berkowitz was "the Master"—but without ejaculating into each other. Perhaps they could just masturbate. And that's what they did. "It was a moment of epiphany," Berkowitz recalled. A startling realization that sex could be "safe, protective, and caring."

As soon as Tom left, Berkowitz sat at his typewriter and typed out a title—"How to Have Sex in an Epidemic: One Approach."

The next day, he shared his epiphany with Sonnabend and Callen. Sonnabend was fascinated, and he encouraged both men to write about ways "to have sex that interrupt disease transmission," including the use of condoms.

Condoms? Neither Callen nor Berkowitz had ever used them. But

Richard Berkowitz, left, and Michael Callen.

why not? And why not now? If the disease was passed through semen and other bodily fluids, it was an effective way to "interrupt disease transmission."

When Callen and Berkowitz began drafting *How to Have Sex in an Epidemic: One Approach*, they agreed to get rid of their earlier language. As they now saw it, promiscuity wasn't the problem. Exposure to body fluids, especially virus-laden semen, was the problem.

With this new emphasis, the two writers invited their readers to be sexually responsible—for their health as well as the health of their partners.

How to be responsible? First, stay sober and in control of your thoughts and emotions. Second, become familiar with the risks associated with each sex act—for example, know that mutual masturbation is less risky than intercourse. Third, talk with your partners about taking precautions that will prevent exposure to each other's body fluids—for example, using condoms during intercourse. And fourth, don't exchange body fluids.

Scraping together $1,000, Berkowitz and Callen printed 5,000 copies of their new brochure and distributed them in gay-friendly places across the city. Writer David France spotted them at a Greenwich Village bar.

"I read through it in one sitting," France recalled. "I wasn't the only patron absorbed in it. The pool table sat idle as a dozen of us passed around copies, hungry for guidance through the terror that sex was causing."

The hunger for advice on safe sex was so widespread that Berkowitz and Callen had to order several more printings. Thousands of copies were distributed across the United States and in Europe.

This wasn't the first safe sex manual to urge condom use in the Age of AIDS. Nor was it the first to use gay-friendly language. In San Francisco, Bobbi Campbell and his friends in the Sisters of Perpetual Indulgence, an all-male group that dressed like traditional Catholic nuns, had published *Play Fair!* The illustrated brochure used camp humor and everyday street language to explain STDs and recommend protection, including the use of condoms.

And before this, back in 1981, the National Coalition of Gay STD Services had published and distributed *Guidelines and Recommendations for Healthful Gay Sexual Activity*, a pioneering pamphlet that employed gay-friendly language to encourage regular testing for STDs and the use of condoms during anal intercourse.

But *How to Have Sex in an Epidemic* was no doubt the most popular of the available options. It saturated gay-friendly areas across the globe, and one of the immediate results was the proliferation of condoms.

"They were everywhere," according to David France. "At doctors' offices, they were given out like lollipops. Jars full of them proliferated at every gay bar and bathhouse. One night on Christopher Street, I watched a team of lesbians on a flatbed truck lovingly hurl the things into the air like rose petals over the heads of their gay brothers."

Safe sex had arrived.

But no one in the White House—which could have saved thousands of lives by supporting a safe-sex campaign—paid attention. In the war against AIDS, the federal government and the administration of President Ronald Reagan were missing in action.

13

THE MISSING WHITE HOUSE

LARRY KRAMER, DRESSED IN A BLUE SHIRT AND MATCHING TIE, LOOKED MORE LIKE A thoughtful college professor than one of New York's most militant AIDS activists. It was 1982. Standing outside the new office of the Gay Men's Health Crisis [GMHC], he fielded questions from a local television reporter. "In the gay community, what is the word that is accurate to describe the reaction to all this?" the reporter asked.

"I don't know if there's one word," Kramer replied. "I think anybody who's got any brain is nervous and scared and concerned. We were looking for an analogy, and someone [said] it's like being in a foxhole. You don't know who's going to get shot down next."

"What have you been able to do for the community?" the reporter continued.

"Oh, we've done everything," Kramer replied. "We've got absolutely no support from any government agency, from any city agency."

The GMHC leader barely hid his frustration and anger. "We've done it all ourselves. We've raised about $100,000, given $50,000 of that away to research. We've put about 15,000 copies [of the GMHC newsletter] out to the public. It is the single most thorough piece of information that has been put out by anyone."

Kramer was just getting started. "We are training doctors how to deal with people who may have life-threatening diseases," he added. "We have support groups for the patients. We have arranged individual therapy for the patients. We are visiting patients in the hospital. We are putting patients together with their families, whom they haven't seen in a number of years, who perhaps didn't even know they were gay. We have a hotline which we train volunteers to man, which is fielding maybe from twenty-five to fifty calls a day from all over America."

He could have mentioned other GMHC services, too, like helping patients fill out their applications for Medicaid. Or he might have pointed to the fast-growing buddy program. Or the legal assistance that GMHC was offering clients who faced discrimination in employment and housing. Or the group's popular educational forums. But the exasperation was setting in. "We don't feel we're doing anything because we're plugging holes all the time," he concluded.

While Kramer explained GMHC's work to anyone who asked, there was one person who scrupulously avoided mentioning AIDS in public—President Ronald Reagan.

✊✊✊✊✊ ✊✊✊✊
F I G H T   A I D S

On October 14, 1982, nineteen months into the Reagan presidency, White House reporter Lester Kinsolving asked Larry Speakes, the president's deputy press secretary, a question about AIDS. It was the first AIDS question ever asked in the White House press room.

"Larry, does the president have any reaction to the announcement, from the Centers for Disease Control in Atlanta, that A-I-D-S is now an epidemic in over six hundred cases?"

"What's A-I-D-S?" Speakes replied.

The answer was disingenuous. It was Speakes's job to stay abreast of the news, and he probably knew about the epidemic.

"Over a third of them have died," Kinsolving said, referring to patients with AIDS. "It's known as 'gay plague.'" Hearing the words "gay plague," the other reporters erupted in laughter.

"No, it is," Kinsolving protested. "It's a pretty serious thing that one in every three people that get this have died. And I wondered if the president is aware of it."

"I don't have it," Speakes said about AIDS. "Do you?" Laughs and snorts filled the room.

"You don't have it?" Kinsolving replied. "Well, I'm relieved to hear that, Larry. I'm delighted."

"Do you?" Speakes pressed on, cracking up the room. "You didn't answer my question. Do you?"

"No, I don't."

"How do you know?" Speakes snapped.

Amazingly, Kinsolving stayed focused. "Well, I just wondered—does the president? In other words, the White House looks on this as a great joke."

Finally, Speakes turned a bit serious. "No, I don't know anything about it, Lester."

"Does the president, does anybody in the White House know about this epidemic, Larry?"

"I don't think so. I don't think there's been any—"

"Nobody knows?"

"There has been no personal experience here, Lester."

Again, the room laughed.

And that was that.

PART FOUR
FROM CARE TO PROTEST

READ MY LIPS

Gran Fury

NATIONAL SPRING AIDS ACTION '88

DAY
1: 4/29-*AIDS and Homophobia:* You are here. Trax benefit 11:30
2: 4/30-*AIDS and PWA's:* 11:30 AM University Hospital, 100 Bergen St. Newark NJ-11:00 AM bus from Center
3: 5/1-*AIDS and People of Color:* Day of Rememberance and Solidarity; Outreach to Black and Hispanic churches.
4: 5/2-*AIDS and Substance Abuse:* Noon, City Hall Demo and Rally.
5: 5/3-*AIDS and Prisons:* 4pm Harlem State Office Bldg., 125th and Adam C. Powell Blvd.
6: 5/4-*AIDS and Women:* Safer sex literature to high school students and Shea Stadium Demo
7: 5/5-*AIDS: A World Crisis:* 4pm International Bldg. Rockefeller Ctr.
8: 5/6-*AIDS Testing and Treatment:* 4pm Demo across from F.A.O. Schwartz
9: 5/7-A **NATIONAL DAY OF PROTEST:** Marches, Rallies and Demos at US capitals. 7am bus to Albany from the Center, 208 W. 13th St. Tickets at Oscar Wilde and A Different Light.
For more info on any of the days call 533-8888

ACT UP / ACT NOW
AIDS Coalition To Network, Organize and Win

"READ MY LIPS." Poster promoting AIDS protests, 1988.

14

TAKING IT TO THE STREETS

"IF THIS ARTICLE DOESN'T SCARE THE SHIT OUT OF YOU, WE'RE IN REAL TROUBLE. IF this article doesn't rouse you to anger, fury, rage, and action, gay men have no future on this earth." In March 1983, Larry Kramer was sounding the alarm again, this time in a front-page article in the *New York Native*. "Unless we fight for our lives, we shall die," he declared.

> There are now 1,112 cases of serious Acquired Immune Deficiency Syndrome. When we first became worried, there were only 41....
>
> After almost two years of an epidemic, there still are no answers. After almost two years of an epidemic, the cause of AIDS remains unknown. After almost two years of an epidemic, there is no cure....
>
> Hospitals are so filled with AIDS patients that there is often a waiting period of up to a month before admission, no matter how sick you are. And, once in, patients are now more and more being treated like lepers as hospital staffs become increasingly worried that AIDS is infectious.
>
> Suicides are now being reported of men who would rather die than face such medical uncertainty, such uncertain therapies, such hospital treatment, and the appalling statistic that 86 percent of all serious AIDS cases die after three years' time.

> If all this had been happening to any other community for two long years, there would have been, long ago, such an outcry from that community and all its members that the government of this city and this country would not know what had hit them.
>
> Why isn't every gay man in this city so scared shitless that he is screaming for action? Does every gay man in New York *want* to die?"

Kramer was part of a new group, the AIDS Network, that had recently enlisted a civil rights veteran to instruct their members in civil disobedience. "We are learning how," Kramer said. "Gay men are the strongest, toughest people I know."

But, for now, the group was holding back. "I hope we don't have to conduct sit-ins or tie up traffic or get arrested. I hope our city and country will start to do something to help start saving us. But it is time for us to be perceived for what we truly are: an angry community and a strong community, and therefore a *threat*."

In San Francisco, the article captured the attention of Gary Walsh, a marriage and family counselor who had Kaposi's sarcoma. "Somebody should do something!" he said.

Walsh soon contacted other gay leaders, including Bobbi Campbell, and began planning a candlelight march that would "honor the dead and support the living." He had once contemplated suicide, but Walsh now had a renewed sense of purpose—he was taking the AIDS fight to the streets.

On the cool evening of May 2, 1983, Dave Marez, a twenty-three-year-old gay man living in the San Francisco area, stood in the middle of the Castro.

Marez had mixed feelings. In this same neighborhood, he had experienced numerous incidents in which he was humiliated and degraded simply for being Chicanx. But the Castro was also home to so many of his gay friends, and tonight it was host to the first AIDS march in San Francisco.

Marez had come to the protest at the invitation of his friend Angel Garcia. As the two looked around, they saw only a handful of gay Chicanx among the thousands of marchers. "The church, family, and just guilt didn't allow many Black and Mexican gay men to share their truth," Marez later explained.

A stark black banner led the march. Carried by Walsh, Campbell, and about ten other people with AIDS, the banner said, "Fighting for Our Lives." Ten thousand people followed. *Ten thousand!* Walsh and his friends had feared that no one would show up.

As the march made its way from Castro Street to the San Francisco Civic Center, Marez could see that some marchers were wearing signs with photographs and the names of people who had died of AIDS. Aside from quiet conversations and occasional shout-outs, the marchers were largely silent.

The mile-long procession ended with a somber gathering at the Civic Center. Five people with AIDS spoke to the crowd. One of them, Mark Feldman, lambasted President Reagan's failure to acknowledge AIDS. "Our president doesn't seem to know AIDS exists. He is spending more money on the paint to put the American flag on his missiles than on spending on AIDS. That is sick."

Feldman also sought to change public perception about AIDS patients. Weary of being called a "patient" and a "victim," Feldman said, "I am defining myself. I am a person with AIDS, a human being." As the crowd cheered, he donned a homemade crown.

Candlelight march, New York City, June 1983.

Gary Walsh spoke with a gentle voice as he praised the community of people with AIDS. "If one of us is sick or needs help, it's one phone call away. . . . And that kind of love and care, to me, is one of the biggest demonstrations of what gay liberation is all about—our deep capacity to love one another."

The Sisters of Perpetual Indulgence passed buckets and collected more than $6,000 to help fight AIDS.

As evening turned to night, David Marez was glad he had come and marched with Angel. At the time, he didn't know why Angel had asked him to attend the vigil, but years later, he learned that Angel, like Walsh and Campbell, had already experienced the first signs of AIDS.

15

PEOPLE WITH AIDS

BOBBI CAMPBELL AND GARY WALSH WANTED SOMETHING ELSE FOR THE FIGHT against AIDS. Like Larry Kramer in New York, they wanted a political organization that would be run *by* AIDS patients and *for* AIDS patients.

Campbell announced the formation of the San Francisco AIDS Alliance. From this point on, he said, the Alliance would demand a voice and vote where decisions about the lives of AIDS patients were discussed, debated, and decided—in politics, medicine, and social services.

Cofounder Mark Feldman, who was close to dying, made sure that the Alliance would also insist that AIDS patients be known as more than just patients. As the organization's statement of purpose put it:

> **BE IT RESOLVED** that we declare that we are not "victims," which term implies defeat, and that we are only occasionally "patients," which term implies passivity, helplessness, and the dependence upon the care of others; rather we declare that we are "people with AIDS," that we are active people, that we are responsible for our own lives, that our strength is through our dignity, that we are fighters, and that we are survivors.

The PWAs—people with AIDS—were ready for action.

Helen Schietinger, a lesbian woman who administered the AIDS clinic at the University of California, San Francisco, had agreed to serve as cochair of the Fifth National Lesbian and Gay Health Conference in Denver. Held in June 1983, the conference would focus on HIV and AIDS. Schietinger thought it was important for PWAs to be present, so in the run-up to the event, she enlisted eleven PWAs to serve on an advisory committee and to participate in the conference's eight working groups. Bobbi Campbell was part of the San Francisco team, and safe sex authors Richard Berkowitz and Michael Callen were part of the New York team.

Schietinger met resistance along the way. Not every medical expert wanted PWAs to have a voice in medical discussions. Best to leave it to the professionals, they said. But she persisted and offered a warm welcome to the eleven PWAs when they arrived in Denver.

Without delay, they made their intentions clear. Yes, we'll go to the working groups, they said, but we'll also meet on our own.

Working together in a hospitality suite, the PWAs felt inspired. "It just fueled us and energized us to realize that this was a moment where we could come up with something to try to make a difference," Berkowitz recalled.

But what could they come up with? Bobbi Campbell and Michael Callen led the way, drafting a document to present to the entire forum. The document drew from their earlier works. Campbell used the mission statement of the San Francisco AIDS Alliance, and Callen used ideas from the safe sex brochure. The larger group loved the final product and decided to present it during a protest at the forum's closing session.

Uninvited, the PWAs rushed the stage at the session, jolting the audience to attention, and unfurled the banner that the San Franciscans had brought with them—"Fighting for Our Lives."

From behind the banner, a PWA began reading the introduction to the document. "We condemn attempts to label us as 'victims,' a term which implies defeat, and we are only occasionally 'patients,' a term which implies passivity, helplessness, and dependence upon the care of others. We are 'People With AIDS.'"

The audience fell silent.

Activists occupy the stage during the closing session of the National Lesbian and Gay Health Conference in Denver, June 1983.

Group members then took turns reading the remaining three sections of the document. The first section called for all people to support PWAs in "our struggle against those who would fire us from our jobs, evict us from our homes, refuse to touch or separate us from our loved ones, our community or our peers, since available evidence does not support the view that AIDS can be spread by casual, social contact."

The second section implored PWAs to practice safe sex and "be involved at every level of decision-making" in educational forums and agencies that provide services to PWAs.

The third section asserted the rights of PWAs, including the right to "full and satisfying sexual lives," the right to "quality medical treatment and quality social service provision without discrimination," the right to "make informed decisions about their lives," the right to privacy, and the right to choose who will visit them in the hospital.

Michael Callen read the last right of PWAs: The right to "die—and live—with dignity."

Audience members leaped out of their seats, and the PWAs lifted their arms in celebration. They had just asserted the dignity that had long been denied them, and they had a clear sense that their document—"the Denver Principles"—would create a better future for PWAs.

On the trip home, Bobbi Campbell dreamed of creating a National Association of People with AIDS, and the New Yorkers plotted how to start their own PWA organization. In subsequent months and years, members of the PWA movement marched in parades, testified before Congress, and published educational literature, all designed to advance the Denver Principles.

Perhaps their most consequential work, though, was demanding a voice in their own health care. Thanks to the Denver protest, as well as subsequent protests, PWAs began to be included in agencies, businesses, and groups that prescribed and delivered health care for PWAs.

But not everyone opened their doors to PWAs, and in the years to come, those folks would feel the wrath of PWAs and their allies.

16

A REVOLUTION ON WARD 5B

KEN RAMSAUER, A TWENTY-SEVEN-YEAR-OLD LIGHTING DESIGNER, HEARD THE TWO nurse's assistants laughing about him. "I wonder how long the faggot in 208 is gonna last," they said.

A short time after the hospital stay, Ramsauer sat for an interview with ABC reporter Geraldo Rivera. He looked as if he had just been knocked out in a boxing match.

His eyes were swollen, his lips were swollen, and his head was swollen. Purple lesions covered his face and neck. "Before I got Kaposi's, I thought I was a pretty good-looking guy, average but happy, and now I see myself fading away," he said.

Ramsauer showed Rivera a picture of himself before developing AIDS. He was handsome, with wavy dark hair, high cheekbones, and a distinct chin. "It's scary I'm not the way I was."

On May 23, 1983, four days after ABC aired the interview, Ramsauer died.

Writer David France attended the public memorial with his friend Ian Horst. "The plaza was crowded with 1,500 mourners cupping candles against the darkening sky," France recalled. "As our eyes landed on one man after another, it became obvious that many of them were seriously ill. A dozen men were in wheelchairs, so wasted they looked like caricatures of starvation."

Horst said the vigil looked like "a horror flick."

Nurse Cliff Morrison saw daily horror scenes unfolding inside San Francisco General Hospital. AIDS patients, many in critical condition, were isolated at the end of corridors. Large warning signs were plastered on their doors, and food trays piled up outside their rooms. Inside, soiled bed sheets were left unchanged, and patients were left unwashed. Some of them cried out—*Help me!*

Fearing for their own lives, many hospital staff members, like those whom GMHC volunteer Rodger McFarlane had encountered in New York, simply refused to enter the rooms of AIDS patients. Those who did go in donned the head-to-toe protection of "spacesuits." *We don't know how AIDS is passed,* they said, *and we don't want to get it.*

There was also open hostility. Some staffers made nasty and homophobic remarks—the kind that Ramsauer had heard.

The crisis in care worsened as the number of patients grew. When staff members suggested creating a separate ward for AIDS patients, nurse Morrison feared that it would become a "leper colony" or a "quarantine area," a place for dumping patients.

So he pitched another idea—a separate ward that would be staffed entirely by people who were devoted to providing care and compassion for AIDS patients. The director of nursing greenlighted the idea, and Morrison got to work.

Sitting in their wheelchairs, the AIDS patients looked at the empty space designated to be the new AIDS ward. "Tell me what you want as a human being," Morrison asked the patients. "Tell me what we should be doing."

"I want to feel like I'm being treated like a person," one said.

While Morrison finalized his plans, critics sneered. "You're probably going to get AIDS," they said. "You're probably going to die."

Morrison admitted that he had fears about the disease. "Yeah," he said, "I might have some anxiety about this, but I am more pissed off and angry than I am scared."

So were the nurses Morrison hired. "We were young, we were straight. We were young, we were old," nurse Alison Moed Paolerico recalled. Their skin colors were just as varied, and some nurses spoke Spanish and English. "And they were all kind of kick-ass—even the straight ones," Morrison said.

On July 25, 1983, Ward 5B—the nation's first AIDS ward—opened its doors and welcomed its first AIDS patients. All were young gay men.

Nurse David Denmark explained to his new colleague, Mary Magee, that nursing on Ward 5B was fundamentally different from nursing elsewhere in the hospital. "You have to get out of the mode that you're here for *curing* people and really get into the mode that you're here to *care* for people."

Cliff Morrison focused on the importance of the human touch. He had read the most recent studies, and he believed what most researchers were saying—that AIDS was probably caused by a virus transmitted through blood or semen. So, in his educated guess, it was probably safe for the medical staff to touch the patients when they would not be exposed to blood or semen.

Morrison called his staff together. "People need human contact," he said. "You know how to do it." The staff nodded in agreement. "We decided that if we can't save these folks, we're gonna touch them," Morrison explained.

FIGHT AIDS

The young gay man wasn't sure what to expect on Ward 5B. Then a nurse walked into his room and touched his hand. He was amazed. "I had no human contact for a year," he later explained. "I didn't touch anybody. I mean, you get numb. You forget things like that. When somebody does touch you, you're like, 'Wow!'"

On Ward 5B, touching meant refusing to wear the spacesuits. It meant applying moisturizer to a patient's hands. And shaving, washing, bathing, and massaging them. It meant holding their hands and giving warm hugs.

Sometimes it meant sitting on a patient's bed and stroking their arm. Or rubbing their feet. Or crawling into a patient's bed and cradling them. Or just holding them tight while they cried out in pain or fear.

Many of the boundaries set by traditional nursing education, with its demand for physical and emotional distance between patient and nurse, melted away. "Here you were allowed to love your patient," nurse Mary Magee said.

Compassion and care took other forms, too. In traditional settings, only family members were allowed to visit patients. But on Ward 5B, *patients* identified who was allowed to visit them. In effect, this meant that patients were visited by their "chosen families"—friends, partners, even dogs and cats.

Patients were also allowed to decorate their rooms with furnishings brought from home—rugs and quilts and lamps and champagne glasses. Twice a month, one fun-loving volunteer, Rita Rockett, threw parties with singing and dancing.

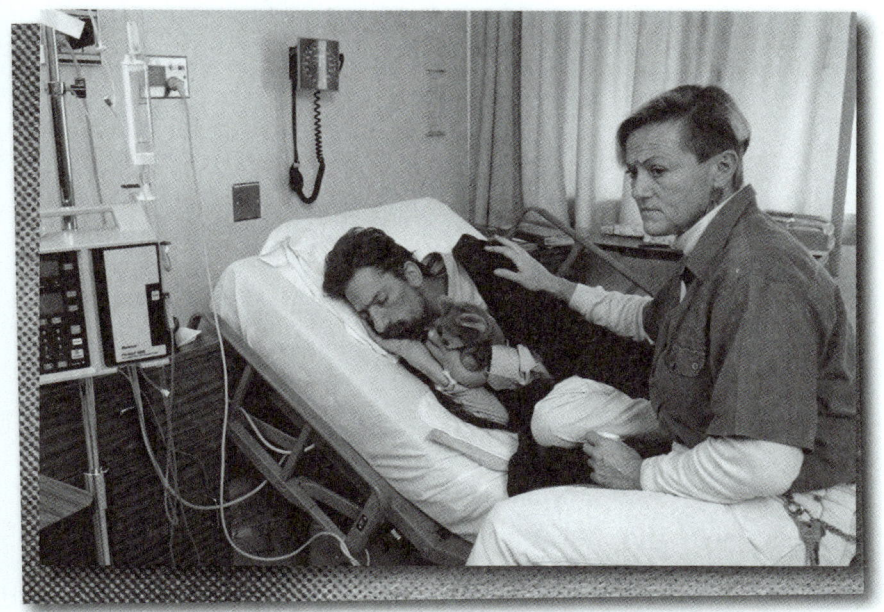

Volunteer and patient in San Francisco General Hospital's Ward 5B.

Lucid patients were encouraged to participate in decision-making meetings about their care, and everyone, staff members and patients, had access to Shanti counselors. Sometimes the counselors would help patients reconnect with families who had abandoned them years before.

On Ward 5B, nurses, counselors, and volunteers sought to assure that no one died alone—that the dying person felt surrounded by a community of care, compassion, and love.

Ward 5B revolutionized hospital care for people with AIDS. Hospitals from across the nation, and the world, sent representatives to learn from "the San Francisco model."

Human touch, it turned out, was remarkably powerful in the fight against AIDS.

17

DYING AND DISCOVERING

GARY WALSH LOOKED THIN, AND HIS VOICE SOUNDED WEAK.

"I can feel it inside," he told Jim Geary of the Shanti Project. "There are all sorts of signs to me from inside that tell me that death isn't far away. It's close."

Walsh had fought hard, but he could fight no more. With the battle behind him, he felt relieved and at peace. Above all, he felt love from those who had stayed close to him in these final days. "Love really is the answer," he said.

FIGHT AIDS

Eight months earlier, Walsh had appeared on a television program with Reverend Jerry Falwell, founder of the Moral Majority, a political organization that advanced conservative Christian values.

Falwell had taken the occasion to depict homosexuality as sinful, and AIDS as God's judgment on gay sex. "When you violate moral, health, and hygiene laws, you reap the whirlwind," he said. "You cannot shake your fist in God's face and get by with it."

"My God is not a vengeful God," Walsh replied, adding that it was perverted of Falwell to use his faith to justify hatred.

"Gary has nothing but my compassion, love, and prayers," Falwell said to the program's host.

"I'm quite a sensitive person," Walsh replied. "I have a hard time feeling that compassion, that caring, and that love for me, given that I'm gay. That does not come across. What comes across is your anger, your hysteria, and your pointing a finger."

Unfazed, Falwell proudly noted that his church in Lynchburg, Virginia, had seven psychiatrists who were committed to "curing" people of their homosexuality.

Now, in his chat with Jim Geary, Walsh looked back on that encounter with Falwell.

Walsh said he had not sensed "one bit of love" from Falwell, and as for the Baptist minister's claim that AIDS was God's judgment, he had three words: "That's just bullshit."

On February 21, 1984, Gary Walsh died. He was thirty-nine years old.

"His legacy was love," said his friend Lu Chaikin.

Two months later, on April 23, 1984, Margaret Heckler, the US secretary of Health and Human Services, delivered history-making news. "The probable cause of AIDS has been found," she said.

The discovery, reportedly made by Dr. Robert Gallo of the National Cancer Institute, meant that the US government now had "a blood test for

AIDS, which we hope can be widely available within about six months," Heckler said. The test would safeguard the nation's blood supply and blood transfusions.

"We'll also be able to promptly and easily diagnose people infected by the virus, and perhaps develop ways to prevent the full syndrome from occurring," Heckler added. Sounding even more optimistic, she said that the discovery would also "enable us to develop a vaccine to prevent AIDS in the future. We hope to have such a vaccine ready for testing in approximately two years."

The implications were mind-boggling. If the nation's blood supply could be safeguarded, if the progression of the virus could be slowed, and if a vaccine could keep the virus from becoming active in the body, millions of lives, in the United States and across the globe, would be saved from the sure and certain death that Gary Walsh had just experienced.

PWAs and AIDS activists were cautiously optimistic, though a staff member of the Gay Men's Health Crisis added, "If a man thinks that he has eight months to a year to live and you tell him that it's going to be two or three years before the vaccine comes out, you know, it doesn't give him a hell of a lot to hold onto."

In France, the announcement created an uproar. A year earlier French virologists Françoise Barré-Sinoussi and Luc Montagnier had identified the same retrovirus, and a heated debate soon arose over who really discovered the cause of AIDS. Not long after Heckler's announcement, researchers proved that the virus Gallo claimed to have discovered was the same one that the French scientists had identified.

Lost in the scientific debate was the contribution of Frederic Brugiere, a thirty-three-year-old gay fashion designer in Paris. Because he had donated tissue samples from his lymph nodes, Montagnier and Barré-Sinoussi were able to discover Human Immunodeficiency Virus (HIV)—the undisputed cause of AIDS.

FIGHT AIDS

Meanwhile, PWAs continued to die, and AIDS activists continued to demonstrate. In July 1984, 100,000 LGBTQ people and their allies gathered in San Francisco's Castro district for a two-mile march to the Moscone Center, the site of the Democratic National Convention. "Holy mackerel!" a spectator declared. "They must have opened up all the closets."

Billed as the National March for Lesbian/Gay Rights, the march was mostly supportive of the Democratic Party. The support stemmed from the party's willingness to welcome lesbian and gay delegates, including Stonewall veteran Mark Segal, and to adopt a policy agenda that favored

National March for Lesbian/Gay Rights, San Francisco, July 15, 1984.

both gay rights and an increase in funding for AIDS research. So the march was celebratory rather than defiant.

But there was also a somber tone. A week earlier, Dr. Marcus Conant had announced a recent spike in the city's AIDS cases. The disease was a "medical nightmare," he'd said.

People with AIDS were a visible part of the march, slowly walking behind the beloved "Fighting for Our Lives" banner. As they drew close to the Moscone Center, where a rally was set to kick off, they could see one of their own on the outdoor stage.

Bobbi Campbell seemed thinner than usual, but his voice was clear and strong when he invited the marchers to join him in a moment of silence for "the two thousand who had died of AIDS . . . and for those who will die before this is over." With his partner, Bobby Hilliard, by his side, Campbell also criticized politicians for conducting "business as usual . . . while we are dying."

"We need increased funding at all levels of government," he said. "We need funding for support services, housing, food, emotional support, home health services, hospice care, and research."

Without mentioning Jerry Falwell's name, Campbell also made sure the massive crowd understood his own beliefs. "Homosexuality does not cause disease," he said. "Germs do! Learn and practice safe sex."

As he concluded, Campbell looked up from his speech text and raised his right arm. "Keep the faith, baby," he said. "I love you."

A few weeks later, Campbell was admitted to San Francisco General Hospital. The doctors tried, but they were unable to tame an infection ravaging his brain.

On August 15, 1984, Bobbi Campbell died. He was thirty-two years old.

Jerry Falwell was still alive, still trying to cure gay men, and still denouncing gay sex. He was also poised to join the bathhouse battles raging in San Francisco.

18

THE BATHHOUSE BATTLES

"HURRY UP, DOC. I WANT TO GO TO THE BATHS TONIGHT."

Marcus Conant was incredulous, and angry, as he completed the examination. *Why would a person with AIDS knowingly subject other gay men to the horrible disease?* But San Francisco's preeminent AIDS doctor felt helpless about the problem. What could he do other than discourage his patients from visiting the bathhouses?

Reverend Jerry Falwell knew exactly what Conant could do: Demand that the bathhouses close right now. The Baptist minister said that because the baths encouraged "the most dirty, vulgar, filthy, bloody occurrences, anal intercourse and worse," and were known to be places where AIDS was transmitted, public officials should immediately shut them down.

Conant was no fan of Falwell, but the doctor eventually contacted Dr. Mervyn Silverman, San Francisco's director of public health, and asked him to shutter the baths.

Silverman was reluctant to close them without widespread support from the city's gay community, so rather than shutting them down, he required them to post warnings and distribute brochures about the dangers of AIDS—an educational campaign that echoed what Perry Brass and the Gay Men's Health Project had done way back in the early 1970s.

Marcus Conant saw the requirement as laughable. *People go to bathhouses for sex, not for education,* he thought.

Gay activist Larry Littlejohn was so frustrated with Silverman that he launched an effort to give San Franciscans a chance to vote on the issue. Littlejohn's ballot proposal, if successful, would prohibit sexual activity in the city's baths.

Just after he announced his plan, more than 200 people turned out for a community discussion hosted by the Harvey Milk Lesbian/Gay Democratic Club. The community was divided, but most attendees opposed Littlejohn's proposal. They condemned it as a futile attempt to legislate morality. An infringement on civil rights. A backhand to the LGBTQ heroes who had fought for liberation. And the beginning of a vicious campaign to close all gay bars, clubs, and movie theaters.

Bill Kraus, a gay congressional aide, offered a moderating view. "I don't want legislation to close the baths, but I do want people to realize that if they continue in these high-risk types of activities, they are fucking fools."

FIGHT AIDS

On April 9, 1984, after months of wrangling with the LGBTQ community, Silverman held a press conference with gay activists and physicians by his side. The public health director announced that he was banning sex in gay bathhouses and other sex-oriented businesses.

"We will be taking steps, with the support of many members of the community, to eliminate the bathhouses, sex clubs, bookstores, as places of sexual encounters between individuals or as a place where multiple sexual contacts take place," he said.

Silverman would enforce the ban by requiring structural changes, like increased lighting, removing doors to the various rooms, and boarding up "glory holes," which encouraged anonymous oral sex. Public health inspectors would also visit the locations and report on their findings. Owners of any place that allowed sexual activity on its premises would be cited, and repeated citations would result in the closing of the business.

Then, on October 9, 1984, Silverman closed fourteen gay bathhouses and clubs. The businesses were "literally playing Russian roulette," he explained. "They promote and profit from the spread of AIDS. Make no mistake about it. These fourteen establishments are not fostering gay liberation. They are fostering disease and death."

Marcus Conant was pleased, but owners of the bathhouses and clubs rebelled. They simply refused to lock their doors. Furious gay patrons also defied the order. Their civil disobedience included having sex at the bathhouses and clubs. A gay activist said that the "baths closure is the first step toward putting us in concentration camps."

Three weeks later, anger against the closure had not abated, and about 300 LGBTQ protesters gathered for a nighttime rally at Harvey Milk Plaza in the Castro. Protest signs were everywhere. "Keep the City Out of Our Sex Lives," "Personal Rights vs. Public Hysteria," and "Today the Bathhouses, Tomorrow Our Bedrooms!"

The fight continued in court, and in late November, Judge Roy L. Wonder ruled that the bathhouses and private clubs were allowed to reopen but that they had to follow strict orders, including the removal of doors on private cubicles.

The judge also ordered the businesses to hire employees to monitor their premises every ten minutes. If the employees discovered patrons engaging in high-risk sexual practices—oral and anal sex that involved the exchange of blood or semen—the patrons must be expelled.

Protestors opposing the closing of San Francisco's bathhouses, fall 1984.

In effect, the judge's order sank the baths.

The closings marked a significant turning point in San Francisco's fight against AIDS. Several more shifts would occur in the following year, and they would affect the entire country.

PART FIVE
TURNING POINTS

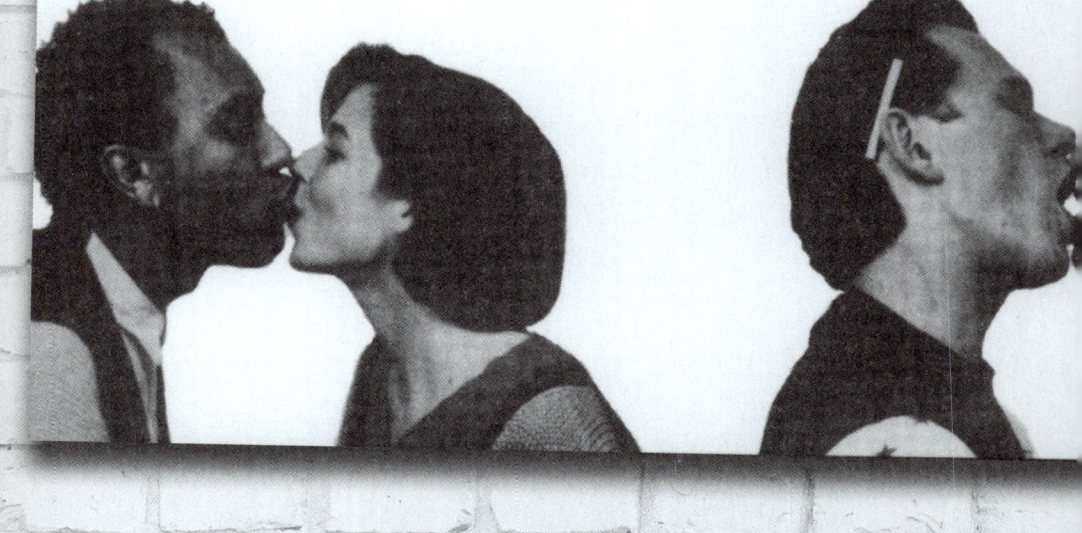

ED AND INDIFFERENCE DO.

"KISSING DOESN'T KILL."
Poster by Gran Fury, 1989.

19

A HOLLYWOOD HEARTTHROB

ON MAY 15, 1984, ROCK HUDSON HEADED TO THE WHITE HOUSE FOR A STATE DINNER honoring the president of Mexico. The fifty-nine-year-old Hollywood star cut a striking figure in his black tuxedo, but his health wasn't quite 100 percent.

Inside the State Dining Room, he mingled a bit and then took a seat next to a friend, Nancy Reagan. "You're too thin," she said. "Fatten up." Hudson smiled and assured her he was fine.

After dinner, Hudson charmed a variety of dignitaries and guests, and the White House photographer snapped photos of him standing with both Reagans, all smiling broadly.

Later that night, another crowd swooned over Hudson—the revelers at Badlands, Washington, DC's, new gay and lesbian nightclub.

For many years, Hudson had starred as one of Hollywood's leading men—romantic, funny, handsome, and heterosexual to the core. But contrary to his onscreen persona, Hudson was gay. He was also in the closet.

The closet door wasn't completely closed, though. Hudson hosted gay pool parties and visited gay bars, nightclubs, and bathhouses, so his

Actor Rock Hudson at a White House state dinner in May 1984, shortly before learning he had AIDS.

sexuality was an open secret among the Hollywood elite and in select circles. Tonight, the LGBTQ clubbers at Badlands were in on it.

FIGHT AIDS

Sixteen days later, Mark Miller, Hudson's personal assistant and friend, grew concerned as he read the mail. Nancy Reagan's social secretary had sent photographs from the White House event, and one of them clearly showed a purplish bump behind Hudson's left ear. Reagan had noticed it, and in a personal note, she urged Hudson to have a doctor check it out.

On June 5, a dermatologist delivered the news. "It's Kaposi's sarcoma," she said.

The star soon traveled to Paris. Michael Gottlieb—a famous AIDS doctor who had coauthored the first AIDS report for the CDC—recommended the trip because of the Pasteur Institute's work on developing HPA-23, an experimental drug for treating AIDS.

During his six-week stay, Hudson received out-patient treatment from Dr. Dominique Dormont of Percy military hospital, but if the treatment offered any positive results, they were not significant.

FIGHT AIDS

Although his health was declining, Hudson accepted an invitation to appear on a hit TV show called *Dynasty*. The pressure of keeping his diagnosis secret almost overwhelmed him when he was in a scene that called for a passionate kiss with actress Linda Evans. Hudson worried that if the two had an open-mouthed kiss, he might infect her with HIV.

But rather than backing out, he did two things. Before the scene, he used lots of mouthwash, presumably to kill any virus, and during the scene, he closed his lips tight and planted them slightly above Evans's lips. The actress found the kiss odd, far out of character for Hollywood's leading man.

"This has been the worst day of my life," Hudson said just after the filming.

AIDS continued to take its toll, but Hudson struggled on. When Doris Day, his longtime friend and costar in blockbuster films, asked if he would help kick off a new cable TV show about dogs, he replied with an enthusiastic yes.

On taping day, which included a press conference, Hudson looked horrible. Photos and clips from the press conference traveled across the globe at lightning speed. Fans and viewers were aghast. He looked so gaunt, so wiry, and what happened to his thick, luscious, dark hair? The rumor mill hit full speed. *Rock Hudson has AIDS! My god, he must be gay!*

Mark Miller urged the star to return to Dr. Dormont at Percy military hospital in France, and in July 1985, the ailing actor flew to Paris, checked into the Ritz, and collapsed. Too sick to remain at the hotel, he was rushed to the American Hospital of Paris.

Dormont wanted Hudson to transfer to Percy so he could receive the experimental treatments that he offered there. But the transfer faced an obstacle: Percy's commanding officer refused to admit the star because he wasn't a French citizen.

Dormont informed Hudson's team that if the Reagan White House or a high-ranking US official made a direct plea, the commanding officer might change his mind. So Hudson's publicist telegrammed the White House and asked for help. After hearing of her friend's urgent need, Nancy Reagan declined to intervene.

On July 25, Hudson's French publicist, Yanou Collart, asked the star to approve a statement she had written. It told the truth about his illness. "That's what they want, Yanou," Hudson replied wearily. "Go and give that to the dogs."

Moments later, Collart spoke to reporters outside the hospital. "Mr. Rock Hudson has Acquired Immune Deficiency Syndrome, which was diagnosed over a year ago in the United States."

Newspapers, television programs, magazines, and tabloids saturated the public with the shocking news. For the first time, millions of people could now say that they knew someone with AIDS.

Parisian doctors soon informed Hudson that his physical condition was too poor and that he would be unable to receive additional treatments.

Deflated, he wanted to go back to Los Angeles, and his team tried to arrange a flight. After several airlines refused to accept him because he had AIDS, Hudson chartered a 747 jet for $250,000.

FIGHT AIDS

That same day, the Reagan administration announced that it was seeking an increase in funding for federal AIDS research. It was the administration's first request for an increase in new AIDS funds. Earlier, increases had happened only at the insistence of Congress—especially Representatives Henry Waxman and Ted Weiss, both of California.

In explaining the 48 percent increase, Margaret Heckler, the secretary of Health and Human Services, said, "Scientific advances on AIDS have been startling and have led to new avenues of research, epidemiology, and prevention activities, which require additional resources beyond those contemplated when the president's 1986 budget was developed."

Critics scoffed at Heckler's statement. New avenues of research had been opening ever since the earliest reports of AIDS, and yet the administration had consistently sought to limit AIDS funding. So what was different now?

The critics had a two-word answer: Rock Hudson. All the publicity surrounding the beloved star, coupled with worldwide expressions of sympathy, had forced the administration, finally, to call for the increase. No longer could President Reagan keep AIDS backstage.

Around this same time, public sympathy was starting to build for another PWA in the news—a teenager named Ryan White.

20

A MIDWESTERN TEEN

"AM I GONNA DIE?"

Ryan White, a thirteen-year-old student at Western Middle School in Kokomo, Indiana, had just received his diagnosis. It was AIDS.

At first, Ryan's mother, Jeanne, wasn't sure how to reply, but then it came to her. "We're all gonna die someday," she said. "We just don't know when." The doctor had told her that Ryan had about six months to live, so someday meant soon, not sixty years in the future, but now wasn't the right time to share that.

Ryan understood what his mom was saying, but he still wanted to pretend that he didn't have AIDS.

On January 17, 1985, forty-four days after entering the hospital, Ryan went home. He spent his time playing video games, watching cartoons, and longing to return to seventh grade. But his weight plummeted to 59 pounds, and Jeanne thought it best to keep him out of school.

After winter, Ryan rebounded. Feeling stronger, he hopped back on his bike, delivered the local newspaper, and played with neighborhood kids. Above all else, he looked forward to starting the new academic year at Western Middle School.

But in July 1985, the school superintendent barred him from

attending classes. "With all the things we do and don't know about AIDS, I just decided not to do it," he explained. "There are a lot of unknowns and uncertainties and then you have the inherent fear that would generate among classmates."

Scientific studies showed that HIV was transmitted primarily through unprotected sex, contaminated needles, and transfusions that

Article from the Kokomo, Indiana, *Tribune*, covering the barring of teenager Ryan White from school, August 1985.

used contaminated blood—which was how Ryan, who had hemophilia, contracted it. But the superintendent focused his worries on saliva. "When you think about students with pencils in their mouths, drinking fountains, lunchroom utensils," he stammered. "What are you going to do about the swimming pool? Should we bar him from that?"

"I'm pretty upset about it," Ryan said. "I'll miss my friends, mostly."

News about Ryan's banishment traveled across the United States, and a national debate ensued. One of the significant effects was that broad sections of the country began to see, for the first time, that AIDS was not limited to gay men and intravenous drug users, that it was also a disease borne by people with hemophilia, even a teenager in Indiana. The country also became more familiar with evidence about the safety of "casual contact" with people with AIDS.

Perhaps the most controversial part of the debate was the frequent depiction of Ryan as an innocent victim. Back in March, Jeanne White had laid the groundwork for this by saying, "The hemophiliacs who get it . . . they're just so innocent. Why Ryan?"

Jeanne's comments implied that other people with AIDS, particularly gay men, were guilty, unworthy of care and compassion. "I'm not mad at them [gay men]," she said. "But if it wasn't for them, Ryan wouldn't have AIDS, so it's kind of hard to meet one, you know. I wouldn't be nasty to them, but I would try to avoid them. I might be nasty to them and not realize it."

But Ryan apparently disagreed with his mother on this point. In his own public comments, he consistently held that all people with AIDS, no matter how they contracted it, deserved to be treated with respect and dignity.

FIGHT AIDS

On August 30, 1985, just after Ryan's school had opened, the Centers for Disease Control finally issued official recommendations on schools and students with HIV. "Based on current evidence, casual person-to-person contact as would occur among school children appears to pose no risk," the report stated. The federal agency recommended that schools consider each case on an individual basis, taking into consideration the student's physical condition, mental abilities, and behavioral issues.

The report did nothing to change the mind of the school superintendent. Like many parents at Ryan's school, he seemed to want scientific evidence which definitively proved that the transmission of HIV through casual contact posed absolutely no risk. The CDC's statement that casual contact *appeared* to pose no risk was simply not sufficient.

FIGHT AIDS

On September 17, 1985, it finally happened: President Reagan publicly addressed AIDS for the first time in his presidency. By this point, about 12,000 US citizens had died of AIDS; the number would double in the following year.

The president spoke of AIDS in response to a reporter who had asked whether he would be willing to support "a massive government research program against AIDS like the program that President Nixon launched against cancer."

Reagan refused to commit, and he defended his administration's financial support for AIDS research, saying it was "a top priority."

The president also weighed in on the national debate about Ryan White's exclusion from school. "If you had younger children," a reporter asked, "would you send them to a school with a child who had AIDS?"

Reagan had prepared for the question in advance of the press conference. "I'm glad I'm not faced with that problem today," he answered. "And I can well understand the plight of parents and how they feel about it. I also have compassion, as I think we all do, for the child that has this. . . . On the other hand, I can understand the problem with the parents. It is true that some medical sources had said that this cannot be communicated in any way other than the ones we already know and which would not involve a child being in school. And yet medicine has not come forth unequivocally and said, 'This we know for a fact, that it is safe.' And until they do, I think we just have to do the best we can with this problem. I can understand both sides of it."

Given an opportunity to support Ryan's wish to return to school, the president refused. Given the chance to support his own CDC, the president refused.

Meanwhile, Ryan suffered in isolation.

21

POSITIVE CHANGE, CREATIVE PROTEST

ON JULY 30, 1985, ROCK HUDSON ARRIVED BACK IN LOS ANGELES AND WAS transported by helicopter to UCLA hospital, where Dr. Michael Gottlieb oversaw his medical care. "He is a very sick man," said Hudson's publicist, Dale Olson. "Everyone is seriously worried."

There were reports that people who had worked with Hudson were also worried. They feared that he had somehow infected them, too. But actress Elizabeth Taylor insisted on going to his bedside. On the way, she asked Gottlieb if it was OK for her to kiss the actor—not because of a threat to her, but because of a threat to him and his immune system.

In September, about 2,700 elegantly dressed people gathered at the Bonaventure Hotel in Los Angeles for a glitzy event hosted by Taylor. It was Hollywood's first major fundraiser for AIDS, and A-list celebrities, including Cher, Stevie Wonder, and Whoopi Goldberg, turned out in full force, all of them inspired by Rock Hudson's decision to go public with his diagnosis.

Onstage, Linda Evans, the *Dynasty* actress who had shared that infamous kiss with Hudson, announced her "love and support" for the dying actor. She had come to believe that by refusing to kiss her passionately, he was trying to protect her from becoming infected with HIV.

Actor Burt Reynolds read a telegram sent by President Reagan that extolled the government's "remarkable progress" in its fight against AIDS. Some audience members hissed loudly.

Hudson also sent a message: "I am not happy that I am sick. I am not happy that I have AIDS, but if that is helping others, I can, at least, know that my own misfortune has had some positive effect."

The stunning event raised more than $1 million for AIDS Project Los Angeles.

A short while later, Michael Gottlieb learned that Hudson was willing to give him $250,000 for whatever he wanted. *$250,000!* The AIDS doctor could have bought a yacht, but instead he created and funded the National AIDS Research Foundation.

The foundation soon merged with an older one based in New York, and with help from Elizabeth Taylor, the American Foundation for AIDS Research (amfAR) became the world's most influential AIDS foundation, raising private funds for research, lobbying Congress for public funds, and advocating for an accelerated process for experimental drugs.

On October 2, 1985, Rock Hudson died.

Randy Shilts, a reporter with the *San Francisco Chronicle*, observed that Hudson's decision to disclose his illness had resulted in a significant turning point in the fight against AIDS. The shift was visible in three areas: "a sharply increased budget for AIDS research, a substantial private fundraising effort for more AIDS studies and, perhaps most significantly, a broadened understanding of the profound threat that the lethal syndrome poses to the health of America and the world."

However significant the turn was, the road ahead still looked long. And dangerous.

FIGHT AIDS

Two days after Hudson's death, a small group of activists in San Francisco gathered outside the federal building that housed the regional offices of the Department of Health and Human Services.

The small protest demanded an increase in services for people with HIV and AIDS, federal approval of AIDS drugs available in other countries, and more federal funds for AIDS research. The demands weren't unusual, but something new and dramatic was taking place.

The activists had secured a one-day permit for their protest, so all was good and legal, but when the permit expired, Steve Russell and Bert Franks chained themselves to a door and refused to leave. Other activists soon brought cots and sleeping bags so that the protesters could spend the night in some comfort.

Then one night turned into two, and two into three, and three into four, with more people joining in and coming and going. Someone set up a table with free AIDS information. The protest was now an encampment—and an illegal occupation of federal property. It was the country's first occupation for the cause of AIDS, and it would eventually become the longest AIDS protest.

Law enforcement officials exercised restraint; they made no arrests and allowed the peaceful civil disobedience to continue without interruption. But in the fourth week of the twenty-four-hour vigil, the peacefulness was shattered.

Three men, one carrying a knife, approached the protesters. "Are you handing out AIDS?" they shouted. "You ought to be dead!" Then they attacked. One man repeatedly struck the face of protester John Hundt.

Activists chained to the door of the San Francisco office of the US Department of Health and Human Services, October 1985.

Another protester sped off to find a phone and call for an ambulance, but the 911 operator hung up on him. Finally, the police arrived, arrested two of the attackers, and sent three protesters to the hospital.

The brutal assault landed in the news, and support for the vigil, in the form of visitors and donations, rose markedly. But the assaults also continued. Sometimes malicious passersby would spit on the protesters. Another time, a group of three men shouted, "Why don't you guys just commit suicide so we can get rid of AIDS?" When a reporter on the scene asked why they would say such a thing, they spewed more hatred. "[We] hate fags, and it's a good way to get rid of them."

But the occupiers continued, and they would soon see thousands of supportive marchers.

22

CORPSES EVERYWHERE

CLEVE JONES AND HIS GOOD FRIEND JOSEPH DURANT STROLLED THROUGH THE Castro, distributing flyers for the annual candlelight march honoring city Supervisor Harvey Milk and Mayor George Moscone, who had been murdered in their offices seven years earlier. Milk was gay, and many believed that homophobia played a part in his killing.

Stopping for a slice of pizza, Jones saw yet another newspaper report about San Franciscans who had died of AIDS. "I wish we had a bulldozer [to raze the Castro]," Jones told Durant. "If this was just a graveyard with a thousand corpses lying in the sun, then people would look at it and they would understand and if they were human beings they'd have to respond."

Jones didn't really want to raze the neighborhood, of course, but he did want the world to sit up and take notice that gay men were dying of AIDS. So he came up with a plan. At a press conference for the march, Jones announced that the demonstration would honor not only Milk and Moscone but also San Franciscans who had died of AIDS. March planners had identified 400 thus far, and they were writing their names on individual poster boards that marchers would carry.

On November 27, 1985, Jones and another friend tucked extension ladders and rolls of tape into the bushes at the old federal building in San Francisco. Jones then met up with Durant, and together they lugged poster boards, markers, and a bullhorn to the start of the candlelight march.

Thousands were gathering at the corner of Castro and Market Streets. "There's a more somber tone this year," a marcher noticed. "I think we're all more conscious of the people who have died of AIDS."

Using his bullhorn, Jones asked marchers to use the markers and posters to write down the names of friends who had died of AIDS. Hundreds came forward.

The march down Market Street began with two people carrying flares. Then came the signs bearing the names of Milk and Moscone, and the rainbow flag designed by artist Gilbert Baker. Three thousand quiet marchers followed, carrying candles and signs.

Seven hundred signs.

Seven hundred names.

Seven hundred dead from AIDS.

At City Hall, Jones gave the only speech of the night. "I stood on these steps the night Harvey and George died," he said. "Like you, I cried. Like you, I have cried a lot since November 27, 1978. I cried for Bobbi Campbell. I cried for Gary Walsh."

Jones abruptly shifted to a scorching critique of all the politicians and medical experts who neglected PWAs. As he ended, his tone was defiant.

"We send this message to America: We are the lesbians and gay men of San Francisco, and although we are again surrounded by uncertainty and despair, we are survivors, we shall survive again, and we shall be the strongest and most gentle people on earth."

Jones then invited the crowd to follow him and take their signs to the federal building where the AIDS encampment was underway. The marchers chanted angrily along the way: "Stop AIDS now! Stop AIDS now!"

Seeing the federal building, Jones used his bullhorn to quiet everyone and share his plan. *We're going to tape our posters—the names of our dead friends—to the front of the building.* The announcement delivered an electric jolt to the crowd. As they moved forward, volunteers retrieved the ladders from the bushes and raised them on the building's façade, not far from the twenty-four-hour occupation.

In a drizzling rain, marchers plastered the posters on the wall. Most were displayed on the first floor, but some appeared as high as the third. Marchers on the ground pointed at all the names, reading them silently or aloud, perhaps realizing for the first time that someone familiar had died.

With the wall covered, the crowd broke out in applause. The deaths of their friends were on full display for the world to see. No longer would they remain hidden, obscured, neglected, forgotten.

Cleve Jones had a vision.

> Standing in the drizzle, watching as the posters absorbed the rain and fluttered down to the pavement, I said to myself, *It looks like a quilt.* And as I said the word *quilt*, I was flooded with memories of home and family and the warmth of a quilt when it was cold on a winter night.
>
> And as I scanned the patchwork, I saw it—as if a Technicolor slide had fallen into place. Where before there had been a flaking gray wall, now there was a vivid picture and I could see quite clearly the National Mall, and the dome of Congress and a quilt spread out before it—a vision of incredible clarity.

On a bus ride back to the Castro, Jones shared his vision with his friends, including rainbow flag maker Gilbert Baker. They weren't impressed. They doubted that he could transform his vision into reality.

"But I was on fire with the vision," Jones recalled.

Meanwhile, about 400 miles southwest of Jones and his friends, in a town not as welcoming of LGBTQ people as San Francisco, discrimination raged on. There, it would center on lesbian women trying to help gay men with AIDS.

23

BLOOD TESTS, BLOOD SISTERS

IN EARLY MARCH 1985, MARGARET HECKLER, THE SECRETARY OF HEALTH AND HUMAN Services, announced another significant turning point in the fight against AIDS—the Food and Drug Administration (FDA) had just approved a test to screen blood for HIV.

The test could not be used to diagnose AIDS, but it could detect the presence of antibodies (the proteins that fight infections) to HIV in a person's bloodstream. If someone had the antibodies to HIV, they also had the virus.

With the new test, blood banks would be able to help safeguard the nation's blood supply. Up to this point, 177 people with AIDS, including Ryan White, had contacted the virus from blood transfusions or blood products.

Six months later, the FDA took another measure to protect blood supplies. It issued guidelines calling for blood banks to refuse donations from men who had sex with men within the last eight years.

FIGHT AIDS

Lesbian activists had long seen donating blood as one way to help in the fight against AIDS. In 1983, Barbara Vick had even cofounded the Blood Sisters, a group of lesbian women in San Diego who designated their blood donations for local gay men. As other Blood Sister groups emerged, they also donated blood to the nation's general blood supply.

In December 1985, Blood Sisters asked the Orange County chapter of the American Red Cross to collect blood at the Gay and Lesbian Center in Garden Grove, California. The blood drive would benefit the chapter, which was experiencing a blood shortage at the time. The chapter agreed, and the Blood Sisters publicized the drive by distributing 500 flyers and sending press releases to local gay and general-interest newspapers. Everything was all set.

But then Dr. Benjamin Spindler, who directed blood services for the Orange County Red Cross chapter, read about the event in his local newspaper and grew so alarmed that he canceled it. When the *Los Angeles Times* asked him why, he said, "We felt that the public was concerned that we might be collecting from gay men, and that is not true."

In other words, Spindler canceled the event because he felt that by collecting blood at the Gay and Lesbian Center, his chapter would give the false impression that it was collecting donations from gay men with contaminated blood.

LGBTQ and AIDS activists cried foul. There had been no public uproar about the event, and even if there had been, Spindler simply could have assured the public that the new blood test had the ability to screen for contaminated blood, or even that the chapter followed FDA guidelines and denied blood donations from men who had sex with men.

Dr. Brad Truax—a friend of the Blood Sisters in San Diego—said Spindler's decision to cancel was "based on blatant homophobia," irrational fear of gay and lesbian people.

Stuart Smith, a leader at the Gay and Lesbian Center, also weighed in. "It [Spindler's act] is discrimination," he said, "but there are no laws to prevent this kind of thing."

He was right about that. There were no laws in Orange County that prohibited Spindler from discriminating against lesbian women who hoped to contribute to local blood supplies.

Spindler refused to change his mind, the blood bank continued to suffer, and the Blood Sisters moved on, still ready and willing to roll up their sleeves and donate their life-saving blood.

Meanwhile, at the National Cancer Institute in Bethesda, Maryland, people with AIDS were also rolling up their sleeves, not to donate blood to the country, but to receive injections of a promising new drug.

PART SIX
FOR DRUGS, AGAINST SILENCE

Enjoy

AZT

Trade-mark®

The U.S. government has spent one billion dollars over the past 10 years to research new AIDS drugs. The result, 1 drug—AZT. It makes half the people who try it sick and for the other half it stops working after a year. Is AZT the last, best hope for people with AIDS, or is it a short-cut to the killing Burroughs Wellcome is making in the AIDS marketplace? Scores of drugs languish in government pipelines, while fortunes are made on this monopoly.

IS THIS HEALTH CARE OR WEALTH CARE?

STORM THE N.I.H. MAY 21. INFO: 212-989-1114

"ENJOY AZT." Poster created by ACT UP to protest the slow progress and high cost of AIDS drug research.

24

AZT ARRIVES

ON JULY 3, 1985, JOSEPH RAFUSE, A FURNITURE SALESMAN FROM BOSTON, HEADED TO the National Cancer Institute (NCI)—which was part of the National Institutes of Health—to take part in the clinical trial of a drug called AZT. Rafuse had already had pneumocystis pneumonia, his immune system was in lousy condition, and he hoped the experimental drug would turn his life around.

Rafuse had no idea how his body would respond to the drug. Would he suffer a seizure? Would he lose control of his bowels? Would his fever spike? Would he die?

The trial was the most significant in AIDS treatment research to date. If successful, AZT would block an enzyme that was essential to the reproduction of HIV—reverse transcriptase.

NCI's leading scientists were present when Rafuse received his injection. They, too, had no idea how his body would react. As the drug coursed through his veins, the scientists monitored him closely. Everyone waited with bated breath.

Whew! Rafuse showed no obvious signs of distress, and he soon headed to a nearby room for further monitoring. Although he developed a fever that night, it did not last. Even better, as he continued to receive

AZT three times a day, his CD4 cells—the white blood cells that help fight infections—started to increase in number and strengthen his immune system.

FIGHT AIDS

The second phase of the trial tested AZT in about 280 PWAs who had already had pneumocystis pneumonia. The twenty-four-week trial required volunteers to stop taking all other medications so that the results would be able to focus on AZT by itself. Volunteers also understood that while half of them would receive an AZT pill, the other half would receive a placebo, a cornstarch or saltwater pill with no obvious health benefits. None of the volunteers would know whether they were taking AZT or the placebo.

Despite the enormous risks posed by going off other medications, and by the possibility of being assigned to the placebo group, researchers had no trouble enrolling enough patients. PWAs were desperate for an effective treatment and even willing to sacrifice their lives in search of one. It was all part of the fight.

The trial proceeded apace until the fourth month, when NCI scientists stopped it cold. Nineteen patients on the placebo had died, and only one AZT patient had died. While AZT appeared to show remarkable results, those on the placebo were dying fast and at a high rate, and the scientists thought it would be unethical for them to continue to administer placebos. Giving placebos when an alternative was available would be like handing out death sentences.

AZT had just become the first drug that appeared to attack HIV directly. It hadn't cured anyone—everyone remained infected with HIV—but those on AZT did not die as quickly as those who had taken the placebo.

There were drawbacks. AZT had proven toxic in a significant number of patients. About half had developed anemia and experienced severe headaches, abdominal pain, nausea, and fevers. The toxicity was so bad that some patients left the trials. Still, those involved mostly believed that the benefits of AZT outweighed its problems.

FIGHT AIDS

On December 3, 1986, seven days after Cleve Jones's vision in San Francisco, the drug company Burroughs Wellcome asked the FDA for approval to sell AZT.

It usually took about a year for the FDA to decide on an application, but just 107 days later, on March 20, 1987, the FDA approved the commercial release of AZT. The speed with which AZT had been tested and approved was shocking. The entire process of testing and approving a new drug typically lasted around eight to ten years, but the process for AZT took less than three years.

What accounted for the fast turnaround? No doubt, the FDA felt considerable pressure from politicians, patients, and activists who demanded AIDS drugs, *right now*, to help all those who were dying. Whatever the reason, though, PWAs were ecstatic about the chance to lead longer lives.

But then Burroughs Wellcome delivered awful news: AZT would cost each patient about $8,000 to $10,000 per year. For many PWAs, especially those without insurance, the price was prohibitive, out of reach. AIDS activists smelled greed—the greed of a company seeking enormous profits on dying PWAs—and they were furious.

They were also livid at the government for failing to test and approve an AIDS drug that seemed to be working miracles in Israel—AL 721.

25

BUYERS' CLUBS

MICHAEL MAY WAS IN A WHEELCHAIR WHEN HE ARRIVED IN ISRAEL. "HE LOOKED LIKE a skeleton," his doctor said. "He was unable to eat and had a fever and skin rash."

The New Jersey resident had traveled to Israel to be part of a study testing an experimental drug called AL 721. May hoped the drug would offer a miracle cure, but deep down, he was pretty sure that he would die of AIDS.

AL 721 was easy to take. All May had to do was to spread it on bread and eat one slice in the morning and another in the evening. After the second week of treatment, May and his doctor noticed marked improvement. His fever was gone, his rashes started to disappear, and his diarrhea was less severe. When he returned to the United States, he was no longer relying on his wheelchair.

In March 1987, the *New York Daily News* published a feature story on May that included a photograph of him appearing to jump out of his wheelchair, his arms spread wide open. The story was captivating, and it left people with HIV and AIDS desperate for AL 721. The problem was that the drug was not approved in the United States.

A drug company in New Jersey had already produced a limited quantity of AL 721, but they were saving it for federal agencies so that they could conduct trials and approve it for use. When activist Michael Callen learned this, he urged the company to release its supply. *PWAs are dying right now, and getting approval from the FDA will take too long,* he said.

The company said no, and Callen was livid. He had refused to take AZT because of its toxicity, and he was hoping AL 721 would save him. Joseph Sonnabend, Callen's doctor, was equally upset—until another of his patients joined the fray.

One day, Stephen Roach, an HIV-positive chemistry student, just showed up at the company's headquarters and, in a surprising turn of events, he discovered that although the company would not share its supply of AL 721, it would teach him how to make it. On the same day of his visit, Roach learned how to concoct a version of the drug.

Back home, though, Roach and his partner, Tom Hannan, discovered that it was too difficult to make the drug on their own. Ingredients for the drug were readily available, but its production required significant expertise. They needed help from an established laboratory, and that required money they didn't have.

So they formed the People with AIDS Health Group. The group's business plan called for soliciting orders for a three-month supply of AL 721 that cost $200. When enough funds were in the bank, the group would sign a contract with a company that could manufacture a drug virtually identical to AL 721.

News about the group's plan spread like wildfire, and $20,000 in orders soon appeared in the group's mailbox. Before long, the orders climbed to $30,000. The bourgeoning list was comprised mostly of people in the middle and upper classes; many poor PWAs couldn't come up with $200.

On May 4, 1987, the People with AIDS Health Group held a press conference where Callen announced that they were all set to distribute AL 721. The group was doing so because of "government indifference and bureaucratic sluggishness," he said. The press conference also included a testimonial from Gary Meckler, who, like Michael May, had received AL 721 from a physician in Israel. Meckler claimed that after taking the drug, his fevers disappeared, and he gained almost fifty pounds.

Hope for good health is what fueled the 150 buyers anxiously lining up at Judson Memorial Church in New York's Greenwich Village. Inside the church, the buyers confirmed their orders and received instructions for handling, storing, and ingesting the orange and slimy drug: *Mold it into small cubes, freeze it, and when you're ready to take it, blend it with orange juice.*

Buyers' clubs like the Health Group popped up in major cities across the country, including in San Francisco. As the clubs distributed AL 721, as well as other unapproved drugs, Callen sought a meeting with Dr. Anthony Fauci, then director of the National Institute of Allergy and Infectious Diseases, part of the National Institutes of Health. Fauci oversaw the federal government's medical and scientific response to the AIDS crisis.

In May 1987, Callen, Larry Kramer, and two leaders from the

Gay Men's Health Crisis met with Fauci and his team of scientists in Bethesda, Maryland.

Callen shared anecdotes of PWAs whose health improved after taking AL 721, and he urged Fauci to conduct more tests on the drug. "It's useless," Fauci replied to Callen. "Our committee considered it. There's absolutely no evidence that it works—*whatsoever*."

Exasperated, Callen also implored Fauci to change his approach to experimental drugs—to consider more drugs faster. "Please, I *beg* you," Callen said. "In wartime, in the trenches, there is a need for emergency medicine. You don't have the luxury of time. The main task is to keep people alive and work out the fine details of science later."

Fauci was unmoved.

FIGHT AIDS

During this period, desperate PWAs also turned to alternative therapies—acupuncture, meditation, crystal therapy, enemas, garlic pills, licorice root, and anything else that might help them fight the disease.

In certain AIDS clinics in Mexico, PWAs received injections of a common cleaning liquid, hydrogen peroxide. Those unable to travel, but hoping for the same treatment, drank water containing a few drops of the household agent.

Mexico also became a destination point for drug runners who bought AIDS drugs that were legal there but barred in the United States. Back in the United States, the runners sold the drugs at exorbitant prices.

But alternative therapies proved ineffective. Just as troubling, early hopes for AL 721 were unfulfilled, and the federal government was still slow to act. Frustrated, AIDS activists were beginning to scream directly in the faces of the researchers and government officials who had failed them.

26

THE MOB SCREAMS

TATTOO THEM!

"Everyone detected with AIDS should be tattooed in the upper arm, to protect common-needle users, and on the buttocks, to prevent the victimization of other homosexuals," journalist William F. Buckley Jr. wrote.

The idea was not a joke, and it evoked fury and outrage from AIDS activists, who quickly called to mind the Holocaust, when German Nazis tattooed identification numbers on Jewish prisoners and required gay prisoners to wear upside-down pink triangles.

Jamie Bauer, the chair of the Swift and Terrible Retribution Committee, the activist wing of the Gay and Lesbian Alliance Against Defamation (GLAAD), decided that her group needed to protest Buckley. And not politely.

On April 30, 1986, Bauer's committee and other GLAAD members descended on the offices of the *National Review*, the political magazine founded by Buckley, in Midtown Manhattan. The protesters wore identification numbers and homemade prison shirts with pink triangles. They carried protest signs and wooden frames designed to resemble prison windows. And they held up fake branding irons with the word "AIDS." Several bold activists entered and occupied the magazine's offices.

It was the type of protest that Bauer and her committee preferred—loud, angry, and in-your-face. Reminiscent of the Stonewall riots. But nonviolent.

Some GLAAD members were less than enthusiastic about the protests, and on occasion the committee saw its plans squelched and killed. Frustrated by the obstructions, several committee members broke away and eventually started a new group—the Lavender Hill Mob.

In February 1987, Michael Petrelis and Eric Perez, two Lavender Hill Mob members, bought gray shirts, pants, and hats at the local Goodwill store. At home, they drew prison stripes on the shirts, sewed pink triangles on the pockets and hats, and stenciled numbers on the sleeves. Then they packed the uniforms and headed to Georgia.

In Atlanta, the CDC was preparing to host a conference on testing for HIV in the general population. The two-day event would be held in the Marriot Marquis and attended by 1,000 health professionals and LGBTQ leaders.

The Mob thought it was the perfect opportunity for a protest. "We're going, and we're going to demand drugs!" activist and Mob member Marty Robinson said.

The CDC wasn't responsible for testing and approving AIDS drugs. Testing was the responsibility of the National Institutes of Health, particularly the National Institute of Allergy and Infectious Diseases (NIAID), and approvals came from the Food and Drug Administration (FDA).

But the Mob didn't give a damn about which agencies did what. As

Lavender Hill Mob flyer criticizing the Reagan Administration's approach to AIDS education.

they saw it, all of them represented a negligent federal government that failed to deliver AIDS drugs.

The Mobsters made their first splash at a cocktail party before the official start of the conference. Dressed in their prison uniforms, Petrelis and Perez shocked the crowd as they handed out protest flyers and wore homemade buttons that said, "Centers for Detention Camps (CDC)."

On the first day of the conference, Robinson attended a session that addressed whether the names of people tested for HIV should remain confidential. But he wasn't interested in the ethics of testing; he was focused on the failure of public health officials to provide effective AIDS drugs.

Taking over a microphone, he shouted about the officials' "inept and murderous response" to the AIDS epidemic. "We will never forgive you for this atrocity!" he screamed. "We will never forgive you for what you've done to us!"

After Robinson's outburst, a woman unknown to the Mob approached the microphone and called upon the government to quarantine all people with AIDS. *Quarantine!*

The Mobsters were irate, and they shouted at the woman until she left the conference room. Michael Petrelis took the moment to tell a reporter why he was in prison garb. "I'm wearing this uniform to protest the Nazi-like tactics practiced against AIDS victims," he said.

FIGHT AIDS

CDC officials favored testing all hospital patients for HIV, saying it would help track and curb the spread of HIV, but by the second day, it was clear that most conference attendees opposed mandatory testing.

Leaders from the established LGBTQ organizations said that mandatory testing, in hospitals or anywhere else, would lead to breaches in confidentiality and widespread discrimination against people known to have HIV. They would lose their jobs, their homes, their health. *Testing should always be voluntary,* they said.

Near the end of the conference, LGBTQ leaders held a press event where they praised themselves for successfully lobbying against mandatory testing. The self-congratulations infuriated the Lavender Hill Mob, and they loudly interrupted the leaders to highlight the urgent need for AIDS drugs.

"You've sold out the gay community!" Michael Petrelis screamed.

"We should be yelling, we should be screaming about this issue!" shouted Mob member Bill Bahlman.

"I think you guys are really out of touch with the gay community,"

Petrelis added. "The anger, the frustration—you're all up there with your nice little suits and ties on and you really don't know what the hell we're going through and all the frustration. After six years there has been no action. And you guys are coming in here and acting as though what has happened today is something to be applauded."

After denouncing the LGBTQ leaders, the Mobsters turned their attention to the closing session of the conference. Mathilde Krim, the coleader of the American Foundation for AIDS Research, asked them not to protest, but they quickly dismissed her as another old, tired voice of the LGBTQ establishment.

Dr. Walter Dowdle, the deputy director of the CDC, was probably not surprised when all five Mobsters leaped on stage during his closing comments. Resigned, he simply stood by and watched as the Mobsters gathered in front of the speaker's podium and unfurled a lavender-and-white banner bearing their name.

"You're just like Nazis," Marty Robinson screamed at the audience. Other Mobsters quickly joined in. "We're tired of the genocide! Stop killing us! Where are the drugs?"

Dowdle waved his hand, bringing the conference to an ignoble end, and walked away.

The protests attracted the attention of major news outlets across the country, including the *New York Times*. Bill Bahlman even appeared on *Crossfire*, a popular CNN program.

In New York, Larry Kramer was impressed. He had left the Gay Men's Health Crisis because it wasn't political enough for his taste, and he saw the Lavender Hill Mob as a better option for the fight ahead. They were militant, they were loud, and they were focused on getting drugs into bodies. Kramer decided to call them.

When the Lavender Hill Mob returned to Greenwich Village, they too were impressed. Someone had put up AIDS posters everywhere, and they were breathtaking.

27

SILENCE = DEATH

JORGE SOCARRÁS WAS AT WITS' END AS HE WALKED THROUGH GREENWICH VILLAGE. More than 100 of his friends had died of AIDS, and the grief was so intense that he wanted to throw himself to the sidewalk, pound his fists on the ground, and cry out. Instead, he took a moment. "I can either do that, or I can try to do something with this energy," he told himself.

Socarrás contacted his friend Avram Finkelstein, whose partner had recently died of AIDS, and the two agreed to meet at a local diner. Another friend, Oliver Johnston, also joined them, and the three chatted about losing partners, the inability of their straight friends to grasp the intensity of their pain, and the fear of becoming sick.

Finkelstein felt so positive about their chat—the chance to share their thoughts and feelings out loud—that he pitched the idea of starting a small group that would meet weekly. Before long, the three men added three others—Brian Howard, Charles Kreloff, and Chris Lione—and they all met for potluck dinners in one another's apartments. They talked about boyfriends, new relationships, who was sick, who was well, but they also inevitably shifted into AIDS politics, AIDS research, and AIDS activism.

FIGHT AIDS

On their first-year anniversary, the group decided to turn outward. Frustrated with the silence still surrounding AIDS, they wanted to activate the streets.

Finkelstein had grown up in the Village, and he knew that "when New Yorkers need to talk to one another, there is always the street." So he suggested that the group make a political poster, like all the antiwar posters he saw in the 1970s, and wheat-paste it across the city. All six group members were artistic, and they immediately rallied around the idea.

Finkelstein then sharpened the idea by saying that the "poster needed ... to stimulate political organizing in the lesbian and gay community, and to simultaneously imply to anyone outside the community that we were already fully mobilized." The group also agreed that the poster should reflect contemporary advertising trends. It "needed to be cool," focused on a gripping image, and light on text.

The group's first idea for a poster emerged in response to William F. Buckley Jr.'s call for tattooing PWAs. But tough questions arose about the ability of a photographed body to represent all the different types of people with AIDS. "Women were coming down with AIDS, black people, black gay people, drug users—it had already crept into so many different areas," group member Chris Lione recalled. "What butt would we use? Would it be a male that was curvy? Would we shoot it in black-and-white so the body would not have a race?"

After lengthy discussions, the group deemed that a photographed body was "inherently exclusionary." They then turned to existing pictographic symbols, including the rainbow flag. But that had its own problems. *It lacks gravitas,* the group said. *Plus, its colors would be unattractive on a poster.*

So which symbol was serious and somber enough to draw LGBTQ people into the fight against AIDS? There was one answer: the pink triangle.

But there was a potential problem here, too. The group thought that the triangle might suggest victimhood. They wanted a powerful symbol that called LGBTQ people to organize against AIDS, not an historical symbol that felt "potentially disempowering."

Nevertheless, the group could not find a better option. "But we gave the familiar symbol a makeover," Finkelstein explained later. Mimicking color trends in 1986, the group changed the triangle's pale pink to fuchsia, a bold color embraced by the edgy New Wave movement in music and fashion.

With the symbol chosen, the group turned to the color for the poster's background. The selection process was rather easy, and the group settled on black simply because so many people in lower Manhattan—artists, designers, writers, musicians—wore black.

The next challenge was agreeing on the text, which everyone thought should be minimal. For an image-driven society, the less to read, at least on a public poster, the better to capture people's attention.

Using a small font, Socarras and Finkelstein wrote and designed the text for the bottom of the poster: "Why is Reagan silent about AIDS? What is really going on at the Center[s] for Disease Control, the Federal Drug Administration, and the Vatican? Gays and lesbians are not expendable . . . Use your power . . . Vote . . . Boycott . . . Defend yourselves . . . Turn anger, fear, pain into action."

Next up was the large tagline that would appear under the triangle—the text and design that people could see even if passing by in a car. In a remarkable burst of pure creativity, the group birthed the slogan in about sixty seconds—"SILENCE = DEATH."

"SILENCE = DEATH." The most recognizable of the many posters and public artworks created to protest and draw attention to the AIDS crisis began appearing on walls in New York City in early 1987.

It had taken about six months, but they had done it. The design process was finished, and the poster was complete. The group soon hired printers and professional wheat-pasters, and in February 1987, hundreds of the posters appeared in the Greenwich Village, Times Square, and Chelsea neighborhoods in Manhattan.

When Finkelstein took the poster to local gay-friendly businesses, some of them refused to hang it, saying that the poster's right-side-up triangle misrepresented the symbol of the persecution of gay men in concentration camps. It was the first time Finkelstein and the group realized that the pink triangle used in the Holocaust was upside down. During the design process, a group member had been assigned to research the triangle's position on the prison uniforms, but he had failed to do so, and the right-side-up triangle had slipped through the process.

Rather than correcting their error, the group decided to own it. To them, the right-side-up triangle distanced the poster from any hint of victimhood. Right-side-up, the triangle was a defiant call to political resistance.

But would it work? Would the poster help activate LGBTQ people to take political action against AIDS? Would it show the outside world that the LGBTQ community was a force to be reckoned with?

The answer was just around the corner.

28

ACT UP!

MICHAEL PETRELIS ANSWERED THE PHONE AT BAILEY HOUSE, A CITY-RUN HOME FOR HIV-positive people. "I'd like to come talk to you," Larry Kramer said, adding that he was impressed with the Lavender Hill Mob.

Petrelis knew Kramer from his off-Broadway play about AIDS, *The Normal Heart*. The 1985 production had been a spectacular hit, earning international attention and high praise from theater critics, including the tough-to-please Frank Rich of the *New York Times*, who described the play's "blood" as "boiling hot." The play's main character, writer Ned Weeks, who sounded a lot like Larry Kramer, scorched everyone who, in his estimation, did not respond to AIDS with urgency—politicians, the media, the medical establishment, and an unnamed AIDS organization that closely resembled the Gay Men's Health Crisis.

Familiar with Kramer's fury over AIDS, Michael Petrelis welcomed his call, and before long, Kramer showed up with a bag of food and two demands: that Petrelis attend a talk he was planning to give at the Lesbian and Gay Community Center in Greenwich Village, and that he bring all his friends. Petrelis asked what the speech would be about. "Don't worry," Kramer replied. "I'm going to say the right things, just come."

Kramer gave a similar order to lots of others, including Andy Humm of the Coalition for Lesbian and Gay Rights. When Humm asked whether Kramer would say anything new or different, Kramer growled: "Just fucking be there!"

Avram Finkelstein saw an advertisement for the talk, and he told his friends that it might be a good idea to go. Maybe it would dovetail with their poster campaign.

FIGHT AIDS

On March 10, 1987, about 250 people, most of them gay men and lesbian women, filed into the main assembly room at the center. Seventy-five lucky ones sat in folding chairs, and the rest stood or sat on the tiled floor. Everyone was curious enough to turn their attention to the impatient man behind the lectern.

As a successful playwright, Larry Kramer knew the power of dramatic speech—words that made people move, metaphorically and

Larry Kramer, co-founder of ACT UP.

literally. "I would like everyone from this righthand side aisle, all the way to the lefthand side of the room—would you stand up for a minute, please?" he said.

Two-thirds of the room stood.

"At the rate we are going, you could be dead in less than five years. Two-thirds of this room could be dead in less than five years."

Shoulders slumped, hearts sank, and stomachs churned as the group sat back down.

"If my speech tonight doesn't scare the shit out of you, we're in real trouble," Kramer said, echoing his earlier writing. "If what you're hearing doesn't rouse you to anger, fury, rage, and action, gay men will have no future here on earth. How long does it take before you get angry and fight back?"

Turning his attention to drugs, Kramer scorched federal agencies, especially the FDA, for making it so difficult to access experimental drugs. "Give us the fucking drugs!" he screamed.

Kramer then lambasted the Gay Men's Health Crisis for failing to protest for drugs, and he praised the Lavender Hill Mob's recent action in Atlanta. "They protested," he said. "They yelled and screamed and demanded and were blissfully rude to all those arrogant epidemiologists who are ruining our lives."

But Kramer wanted something bigger than the Lavender Hill Mob. He wanted the various LGBTQ groups to join with new activists in creating a "central organization" that would stage nonviolent direct-action protests for access to drugs. "We have to go after the FDA—fast," he said. "That means coordinated protests, pickets, arrests."

Kramer's impassioned plea stirred the audience, and they enthusiastically backed his call for a militant campaign.

Two days later, about 350 LGBTQ folks streamed into the expansive dining room at Bailey House. Primed for protests, they offered numerous ideas. *Stop the subways! Occupy the Statue of Liberty! Block the tunnels! Shut down the FDA!*

Cofacilitator Vivian Shapiro, a well-known and trusted lesbian activist, suggested that the group begin with a picket line at the corner of Wall Street and Broadway. Like many others, Shapiro was livid about the exorbitant cost of AZT, the pharmaceutical industry's slow response to AIDS, and the federal government's foot-dragging in releasing new drugs. Shapiro wanted *more drugs, more better drugs, and more better drugs faster!*

A majority vote settled it—the first protest would be on Wall Street, home to the New York Stock Exchange and its pharmaceutical members, and the theme would be "no more business as usual."

A few days later, while the group was planning the demonstration, they realized they needed a name. A strong name. One that captured their identity. Their mission.

Michael Petrelis suggested "CAN, Cure AIDS Now," but that lacked sufficient fire power. Tim Sweeney, a leader of the Gay Men's Health Crisis, proposed the "AIDS Coalition of New York," but that was too staid.

Steven Bohrer, a young man in a trench coat, said that he had long thought that a great name for an activist group would be "ACT UP." Together, the group fleshed out what the letters would stand for—the "AIDS Coalition to Unleash Power."

Someone grumbled that "ACT UP" sounded like a toothpaste brand, but a majority vote settled it—Bohrer won.

ACT UP's members then split into working groups. They designed posters, thought up chants, and drew up a wide-ranging list of demands: "Immediate release by the federal Food & Drug Administration of drugs that might help save our lives. Immediate availability of these drugs at affordable prices. Curb your greed! Immediate massive public education to stop the spread of AIDS. Immediate policy to prohibit discrimination in AIDS treatment, insurance, employment, housing. Immediate establishment of a coordinated, comprehensive, and compassionate national policy on AIDS."

FIGHT AIDS

On March 24, 1987, just as the morning rush hour was starting, hundreds of activists descended on Wall Street for ACT UP's first protest. Many of them carried the eye-catching posters that Finkelstein and his friends had donated—"SILENCE = DEATH."

"We are angry, we want action!" the protesters yelled. "Release those drugs! Release those drugs!"

"We're basically protesting the fact that the government is sitting on eight drugs that are more promising . . . than AZT," Larry Kramer told a reporter. As he spoke, protesters hanged and burned an effigy of FDA director Ralph Young.

Kramer added that ACT UP also wanted the FDA to demand a lower price for AZT. "Such greed on the bodies of dead people is really gross," he said.

At 8:00 a.m., seventeen protesters sat down in the middle of the street, at the intersection of Wall Street and Broadway. Angry drivers yelled and blasted their horns, all to no avail. When the protesters saw police officers walking toward them, they laid down, refusing to budge. Eventually, the officers pushed and pulled them onto stretchers and hauled them away. Mark Aurigemma, one of the seventeen arrested, said, "Getting arrested is nothing—people are dying from AIDS."

ACT UP had arrived. It was loud, direct, confrontational. It was the nonviolent spirit of Stonewall. And it would challenge anything that obstructed it from winning access to AIDS drugs and justice for everyone with HIV and AIDS.

In San Francisco, Cleve Jones was planning for a much quieter demonstration.

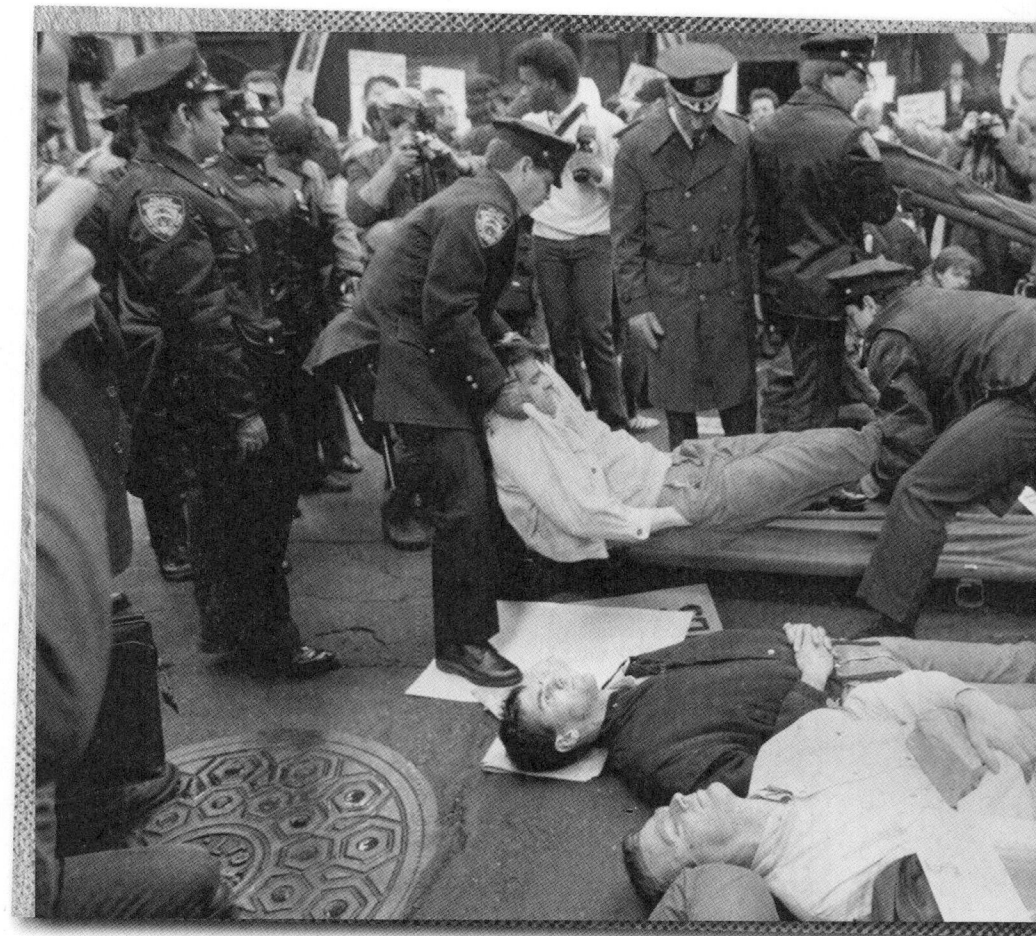

ACT UP protest at Broadway and Wall Street, New York, March 24, 1987.

PART SEVEN
COMFORT AND CHALLENGE

"AIDSGATE." Poster by the SILENCE = DEATH collective protested the absence of political leadership in addressing the AIDS crisis—specifically from the administration of President Ronald Reagan.

29

THE AIDS QUILT

CLEVE JONES STILL DREAMED OF A MASSIVE AIDS QUILT, BUT TONIGHT HE HAD something else in mind—two neo-Nazi skinheads standing in front of him. Jones avoided making eye contact as he walked by, but he heard them loud and clear. "Too many goddamn queers in Sacramento."

In a matter of seconds, one of the skinheads lunged, knifing Jones in the shoulder. As he lay writhing on the ground, both skinheads kicked him furiously. "Faggot, faggot, faggot," they screamed. Then they disappeared into the night, leaving Jones with blood spurting out of his shoulder.

News of the stabbing made the front page of the *Sacramento Bee*. "It was just random anti-gay violence and there's more of this going on," Jones told the reporter.

Randy Schell, a spokesperson for San Francisco's Committee United Against Violence, confirmed Jones's point. "Gay people have always been subject to assaults," he said. "Now with AIDS, it's almost as though [all gay people] are diseased. This translates to people that it's OK, even noble, to go and assault gay people."

The knife wound was not life-threatening, but it left emotional scars. "I was consumed with hatred and fear of heterosexuals," Jones said later.

Adding to the emotional turmoil was news that his best friend, Marvin Feldman, was dying of AIDS. Jones flew to Feldman's family home in Rhode Island, and he was able to climb into Feldman's bed and hold him and talk with him before he lapsed into a coma.

While that helped both, it didn't ease the pain when Feldman died. "I felt like a rat in a cage with all the gates closing and no means of release," Jones said.

In February 1987, release came as Jones and friend Joseph Durant began cutting soft cloth into panels measuring three feet by six feet—the size of a grave. It was the start of the AIDS Quilt. Each panel would bear the name of a friend or acquaintance who had died of AIDS. Thus far, their list numbered about forty.

Cleve Jones with the first panels of the AIDS Quilt, 1987.

Jones quickly settled on the name for his first panel—Marvin Feldman. Using stencils, he spray-painted Feldman's name in black and surrounded it with pink and blue Stars of David.

Making the panel helped channel all the fury and fear that Jones had built up in the past year. "Something about working with the fabric, the paints, thinking about him and not crying—it really helped," he said.

But before long, Jones and Durant started to bicker about how to display the quilt. Durant wanted it to be on scaffolding, and when Jones insisted that it be displayed on the ground so mourners could kneel and touch it, Durant quit.

Others came aboard. Ronald Cordova agreed to be technical director, overseeing the quilt's assembly. The plan was to sew together individual panels into twelve-foot squares that would be laid out, on the National Mall in Washington, with walking paths between them. The paths would allow mourners to get close to the panels of their loved ones.

Michael Smith signed up to take care of business matters, though there was little to manage in the early months. At the quilt team's first public meeting, only two people showed up. The good news was that both had made quilts.

Finally, in the summer of 1987, the project started to take off. The quilt attracted lots of positive attention during Pride Week in June, and the work—now called the NAMES Project AIDS Memorial Quilt—moved into a storefront building in the Castro.

"People just started walking in carrying pens, pencils, industrial sewing machines," Michael Smith said. "This is a way to get over the fear, the sadness, and the paralysis."

Feature stories in national newspapers and magazines, including *People*, soon followed, resulting in a flood of quilt panels. By early October, the workshop had received 1,920 panels. One man dying of AIDS had made and sent his own.

The plan was to place the quilt on the National Mall in October. With one week remaining until the quilt left for Washington, volunteers spent twelve hours a day sewing the panels together into the twelve-by-twelve squares.

On October 11, 1987, Cleve Jones and 500 volunteers arrived at the National Mall around 2:00 a.m. Working by flashlight, the team laid out cloth walkways and placed the folded quilt squares inside them.

Someone asked volunteer Mary Jane Edwards—president of Mothers of AIDS Patients—whether her ill son would see the quilt on television.

"No," Edwards replied, tears welling in her eyes. "They're taking him off the truck. That woman over there is holding him in her arms and laying him down."

Just after the break of dawn, Cleve Jones stood at a microphone for the public reading of the names on the Quilt. "Marvin Feldman," he began.

Hundreds watched from the perimeter of the grid as volunteers unfolded the first square. Jones choked back tears, his voice cracked, and after he finished his list, he walked far away, sobbing.

The next reader began, and about sixty others waited for their turn. The mood was mostly sober and mournful, but actor Robert Blake shared his "outrage that there should be even one panel let alone thousands."

The reading went on for at least two hours, and as it ended, volunteers unfolded the last square. Now on full display, the AIDS Quilt looked massive, about two football fields long, and soft and billowy. Comforting.

The AIDS Quilt laid out on the National Mall in Washington, DC, October 11, 1987.

Tim Brown took his time as he walked along the pathways. "It's pretty painful," he said. "I suppose everyone with AIDS is wondering whether their name will be read somewhere."

It took a while, but Mike Trummer eventually found it. Kneeling, he gently spread his late partner's ashes over the panel bearing his name.

Suzanne Fried sobbed as she knelt next to the panel for her brother, Richard Bruce Fried, who had worked for Walt Disney Productions. "Life's not supposed to be this way," she cried. "We're all supposed to grow old together."

Some of the panels were flashy and flamboyant. Rock Hudson's had stars and a rainbow, and the musician and entertainer Liberace's had a gold background and embroidered illustrations of his piano and candelabra. Some panels were plain and simple, showing only a name or initials written with a marker.

The panel for Stephen Roach—who had tried to make a batch of AL 721 after visiting Praxis Pharmaceuticals—was blue, the color of his eyes.

Twenty-two panels were anonymous. One of them said, "I have decorated this banner to honor my brother. Our parents did not want his name used publicly. The omission of his name represents the fear of oppression that AIDS victims and their families feel."

Lots of panels had personal mementos sewn onto them. Cleve Jones saw "locks of hair, record albums, souvenir postcards, a Barbie doll, whistles, crystals, a motorcycle jacket, a tuxedo, a shard of glass, foam-rubber french fries, toy cars, a thimble, a cowboy hat, teddy bears, a Lacoste shirt, a Buddhist's saffron robe, and even a padded jock."

Although most panels memorialized gay men, some were tributes to those from other groups. There was a panel for "Nancy," an intravenous drug user. A panel for a four-year-old boy pictured a rising sun and the lyrics of "You Are My Sunshine." The one for Baby Jessica featured her stuffed animals, including a precious yellow bunny tucked under a blanket.

"This is simultaneously one of the most beautiful and most horrible things I've ever seen," a man told Jones.

Thousands of people visited the quilt that day, and major news media across the country and globe reported on the event.

Not everyone appreciated the quilt. Some ACT UP members saw it as too quiet, too passive, too weak, an entirely insufficient response to the AIDS crisis. But Jones said that he had never claimed that the quilt was the best way to respond to the crisis. "It's one response among thousands, not the final answer."

Later that day, another response took place—the National March on Washington for Lesbian and Gay Rights.

30

THE LARGEST PROTEST

NINETEEN PWAS IN WHEELCHAIRS LED THE NATIONAL MARCH ON WASHINGTON FOR Lesbian and Gay Rights. One carried a homemade sign that said, "I have AIDS. Please hug me. I can't make you sick."

Hundreds with HIV and AIDS, as well as their friends and families, fell in line behind those in wheelchairs. The sight of so many people with HIV and AIDS gave the march a solemn tone. "For some of these people, it's their last chance, no doubt," a marcher observed. "Someone will die tomorrow who's marching today."

By contrast, the sight of the White House evoked white-hot anger. As the marchers passed by, they jabbed their fingers and shouted, "Shame, shame, shame!"

The activists were still angry with President Reagan for ignoring the disease in his first five years in office. They were also peeved about the new Presidential Commission on the Human Immunodeficiency Virus Epidemic.

Commission members included people who had little or no expertise in AIDS, and several held opinions that activists found repugnant. One opposed the use of condoms, another favored mandatory HIV testing, and another opposed AIDS education in schools.

People with AIDS at the head of the National March on Washington for Lesbian and Gay Rights, October 11, 1987.

About 200 ACT UP members added to the outbursts at the White House. "Act up!" they shouted. "Fight back! Fight AIDS!"

The activists carried posters, made by the SILENCE = DEATH collective, that featured a black silk-screened image of President Reagan with bloodshot eyes, except the blood was hot pink.

The shocking poster also included the word "AIDSGATE," a reference to the Watergate scandal that had brought down the presidency of Richard Nixon.

"This Political Scandal Must Be Investigated!" the bottom of the poster read. "54% of people with AIDS in NYC are Black or Hispanic... AIDS is the No. 1 killer of women between the ages of 24 and 29 in NYC... By 1991, more people will have died of AIDS than in the *entire* Vietnam War... What is Reagan's real policy on

AIDS? Genocide of all Non-Whites, Non-males and Non-heterosexuals? . . . SILENCE = DEATH."

President Reagan wasn't at the White House during the march. He was at Camp David, the presidential retreat in Maryland.

After marching, the 400,000 demonstrators rallied behind the US Capitol. It was the largest AIDS-related protest to date. Leader Virginia Apuzzo—a cofounder of the Human Rights Campaign Fund—angrily criticized the Reagan administration's response to AIDS. "How many more people must die for this administration to wake up?" she asked.

Actress Whoopi Goldberg wondered whether the president cared about the Ray brothers, three HIV-positive children with hemophilia whose home was recently destroyed by fire. Many suspected arson. "Mr. President, did you send them a letter of condolence?" Goldberg asked.

FIGHT AIDS

The following Tuesday, Sally Eckington, a lesbian activist from Oakland, California, participated in a massive civil rights demonstration at the US Supreme Court. Earlier, she had decided not to get arrested, but then she saw the AIDS Quilt, and marched past the White House, and rallied outside the Capitol. Now, she was fired up.

Eckington was one of 5,000 demonstrators at the Supreme Court. Most were protesting a recent ruling that upheld the criminalization of oral and anal sex, but AIDS activists, including ACT UP members, were also there. So were 150 police officers in riot gear, night sticks in hand.

Wearing shirts with the "SILENCE = DEATH" logo, the AIDS activists slipped past the police barricades and headed toward the steps leading to the Court's entrance. At the plaza just in front of the steps, they sat down, linked arms, and began their chant: "We have AIDS, and we have rights."

It was a peaceful protest, so the officers didn't strike anyone with their nightsticks, but they did make sure to don white surgical gloves, reportedly to avoid being infected with HIV. The protesters mimicked them by putting on yellow rubber gloves, the kind used for cleaning toilets.

Protester Hillel Gray took the occasion to educate the police about HIV and AIDS. "It is blood and semen you have to look out for," he explained. "A lot of us may be infected, but it is a preventable disease. There is nothing for you to be afraid of."

By the end of the six-hour-long protest, about 600 activists, including Sally Eckington, had been arrested. It was the largest act of civil disobedience at the Court since the Vietnam War protests in May 1971.

As the several days of protest ended, Cleve Jones offered a summary: "The events all fit together. The march signified our strength and numbers. The quilt signified the depth of our pain, and this [civil disobedience] shows our determination to fight back with every means at our disposal short of violence."

31

RYAN WHITE TESTIFIES

THE HEARING ROOM FOR THE PRESIDENTIAL COMMISSION ON HIV WAS PACKED.

"Because of a lack of education on AIDS," Ryan White testified, "discrimination, fear, panic, and lies surrounded me."

He recounted the shocking details, too—"the lies about me biting people, spitting on vegetables and cookies, urinating on bathroom walls."

The commission was spellbound.

FIGHT AIDS

A year earlier, White and his family were living in Kokomo, Indiana. The taunts he suffered there were so vicious that he told his mother, Jeanne, that he didn't want to be buried in the town.

Hearing that heartbreaking revelation, Jeanne packed up the house and moved the family to the nearby town of Cicero, where, if all went well, Ryan would attend Hamilton Heights High School.

Principal Tony Cook decided to learn everything he could about HIV and AIDS. Armed with the basic facts, he admitted Ryan to Hamilton Heights and assured him that he would be able to use the

Ryan White.

same bathrooms, water fountains, and dinnerware available to all other students. He would even be able to attend physical education classes.

Cook also gave numerous educational talks to students, teachers, and the wider community. He supplied the school library with AIDS educational material. He trained staff for potential emergencies. And he recruited student leaders to inform their peers that AIDS was not transmitted through casual contact.

On the first day of school, Principal Cook shook Ryan's hand and welcomed him to Hamilton Heights. The school community, though

RYAN WHITE TESTIFIES

steeped in AIDS education, wasn't entirely free of nervousness and anxiety, and Ryan decided that he, too, would help.

"When he [Ryan] first came, a lot of people were really scared," a former classmate recalled. "But Ryan helped all of us to understand. He didn't want people to feel sorry for him. He hated that. He just wanted to be a regular kid."

FIGHT AIDS

Ryan shared his positive update with the presidential commission. "For the first time in three years, we feel we have a home, a supportive school, and lots of friends," he said.

"I'm just one of the kids, and all because the students at Hamilton Heights High School listened to the facts, educated their parents and themselves, and believed in me. Hamilton Heights is proof that AIDS education in schools works."

US Navy Admiral James Watkins was the new chair of the presidential commission, and he made sure to include Ryan's recommendation in his notes.

FIGHT AIDS

Surgeon General C. Everett Koop—the country's leader in public health—believed that AIDS education in private homes could work, too. Three months after Ryan's testimony, Koop mailed 117 million copies of *Understanding AIDS*, an educational booklet, to every known home address in the United States. It was the largest educational campaign about HIV and AIDS to date.

Koop was one of the very few officials in the Reagan administration who spoke of AIDS in frank and explicit terms. In 1986, he had written a report that said abstinence *and condoms* were the best ways to prevent the spread of AIDS.

His recommendation of condoms earned the wrath of prominent leaders in the administration who opposed anything but calls for abstinence. As Koop later explained, "The White House doesn't like the C word. But if you don't talk about condoms, people are going to die."

The new booklet, *Understanding AIDS*, talked about condoms. It said that "condoms have been shown to help prevent the spread of sexually transmitted diseases," and it recommended their use to stop the spread of HIV. Reagan did not mention the book publicly, but many of his supporters, including Jerry Falwell, loudly denounced it as morally bankrupt.

As the mass mailing arrived in homes, AIDS activists wondered about the forthcoming report of the presidential commission.

Earlier, Admiral Watkins had surprised the Reagan administration by criticizing it for failing to provide sufficient funding for the Food and Drug Administration. The lack of funds left him "embarrassed," he said.

Watkins's comments had pleased Lavender Hill Mob activist Bill Bahlman. With support from ACT UP, he had been attending commission meetings and providing members with a steady diet of research findings and critiques of the federal response to AIDS. His help was well received, especially by the commission's executive director.

In early June 1988, Admiral Watkins released his draft report. It was sharply critical. Watkins faulted the Reagan administration, though not by name, for a "distinct lack of leadership and coordination" that "resulted in a slow, halting and uneven response."

But the report was constructive, too. Watkins recommended that President Reagan declare AIDS to be a national health emergency and give the surgeon general all the powers required for coordinating a national campaign against HIV and AIDS.

The centerpiece of the admiral's report addressed the issue of discrimination against people with HIV. Watkins described discrimination as "the most significant obstacle" that the federal government faced when trying to track and control the epidemic. "People will simply not come forward to be tested, or will not supply names of sexual contacts for notification, if they feel they will lose their jobs and homes," Watkins wrote.

Because discrimination was such a massive problem, Watkins called upon Reagan to support the passage of a federal law prohibiting discrimination against anyone with HIV and to issue an executive order banning such discrimination in the federal government.

Watkins's report also included hundreds of recommendations on virtually all aspects of the epidemic, not just research but also education, prevention, social and legal issues, and others. For the admiral, solving the AIDS epidemic required much more than focusing on HIV alone.

AIDS activists, medical workers, and social workers agreed, and they were delighted to see that Watkins recommended so many things they had been advocating for—improving the quality of basic health care for PWAs; including PWAs on advisory committees on drug trials; speeding up the process of testing and approving drugs; combatting rising HIV infections among women, people of color, and intravenous drug users; increasing financial assistance for indigent PWAs; and educating K-12 students about HIV and AIDS. The admiral even singled out praise for the Community Research Initiative in New York City, a group of neighborhood doctors and AIDS patients who were so frustrated with the federal government that they conducted their own trials of potential AIDS drugs.

Activists were generally thrilled with Watkins's work, especially his call for the government to spend $3 billion for a national AIDS campaign. But how would President Reagan react? That was perhaps the most important question at this point.

"I believe the White House is going to like it," Watkins said.

At the end of June 1988, Watkins delivered the final report to the White House. If President Reagan liked the recommendations, he did not say so.

Refusing to comment on the report's specifics, Reagan merely said, "The report embraces the major concepts my Administration laid out over a year ago: to be compassionate toward victims of the disease; to care for them with dignity and kindness, and at the same time to inform and educate our citizens so that we can prevent the further spread of the disease."

Nor in the months ahead did the president act as if he liked the recommendations. He did not declare AIDS to be a national emergency. He did not empower the surgeon general to lead a national campaign against AIDS.

He did not back a federal law banning discrimination against HIV-positive people. He did not issue an executive order banning discrimination in federal government.

He did not call for teaching AIDS to K-12 students. And he did not support putting $3 billion into the AIDS fight.

President Reagan opposed, undermined, or otherwise ignored Admiral Watkins's recommendations. Watkins did not further criticize the president, but for many AIDS activists, the president's response was yet more evidence that they had to become more militant in the fight against AIDS.

PART EIGHT
ACT UP!
FIGHT BACK!
FIGHT AIDS!

"STORM THE NIH." Poster created by ACT UP targeting the administration of President George H. W. Bush and advertising a protest at the National Institutes of Health.

32

SEIZE CONTROL OF THE FDA!

NO ONE AT ACT UP UNDERSTOOD AIDS DRUGS BETTER THAN IRIS LONG. ARMED WITH a PhD in pharmaceutical chemistry, she jump-started a small group that studied drugs and monitored experimental drug trials.

The group eventually became the Treatment and Data Committee (T+D), and its purpose was to identify safe and effective AIDS drugs and to pressure the federal government to approve the testing and sale of those drugs.

Long was not a fan of buyers' clubs and drug runners. She argued that AIDS activists would be far better off, in terms of accessing safe and effective drugs at affordable prices, by forcing the Food and Drug Administration (FDA) and the National Institutes of Health (NIH) to identify, test, and approve promising drugs with all due speed.

Fellow activist Greg Bordowitz could not have agreed more.

FIGHT AIDS

"We need to seize control," Bordowitz said.

It was June 13, 1988, and the ACT UP New York meeting was growing intense. Bordowitz had just detailed the FDA's failures to approve and deliver experimental drugs on a speedy basis. Now he called for activists from around the country to descend on the FDA, seize control, and demand radical changes.

Bordowitz and fellow ACT UP member Robert Garcia packed their bags and pitched the idea to other ACT UP groups that had formed in major cities across the country: ACT UP Chicago, ACT UP San Francisco, ACT UP Houston, and more. Meanwhile, ACT UP New York planned an inside-outside strategy for the campaign. T+D committee member David Barr sought meetings with the FDA, while others plotted a direct-action, nonviolent protest at FDA headquarters in Rockville, Maryland.

In face-to-face meetings, Barr and others presented FDA officials with a list of ACT UP's demands: Include us in your decision-making. Add women, people of color, drug users, and children to drug trials. Force private drug companies to release their drugs at affordable prices.

And speed up the approval process—now!

The meetings did not translate into any promises from the FDA, so the protest was on.

On October 11, 1988, about 1,000 ACT UP members descended on the FDA building from a nearby hill. They blasted airhorns, they carried protest signs, and they shouted at the top of their lungs. "Act up! Fight back! Fight AIDS!"

As the marchers surged toward the building, about 250 police officers wearing riot gear and latex gloves protected the entranceway. Police and news helicopters hovered above. Louder and louder, the protesters chanted: "AZT is not enough! Give us all the other stuff!"

A group of protesters called the Delta Queens surrounded the flagpole and hoisted a flag that read "75,000 People with AIDS Fight Back."

"Drugs for sale!" shouted a protester. His group had set up a makeshift store to sell dextran sulfate, an increasingly popular drug among PWAs. "Unapproved by the FDA! We're selling it anyway!" they yelled.

Somehow, activist Peter Staley climbed on top of the entranceway's overhang and hung a black "SILENCE = DEATH" banner. The crowd below roared. "Seize control! Seize control!"

Vito Russo, a well-known gay leader, spoke at a press conference while the protest raged on. "We're not asking the FDA to release dangerous drugs, without safety or efficacy," he explained. "We are simply asking the FDA to do it quicker."

Russo was HIV-positive, and he did not look well. "I'm here today because I don't want my name on a quilt in front of the White House," he said.

Nearby, a protester held a sign—"Time Isn't the Only Thing FDA Kills." A group called the Tombstoners added to that message by lying down and placing cardboard tombstones behind their heads. "AZT Wasn't Enough," one said.

Other tombstones criticized the FDA for failing to conduct trials with women and people of color, and members of ACT UP's Women's Caucus and Majority Action Committee also passed out flyers saying, "We recognize that every AIDS death is an act of racist, sexist, and homophobic violence."

Back at the flagpole, a group raised an effigy of President Reagan. "Guilty! Guilty! Guilty!"

Officers arrested protesters who refused to leave restricted areas, or threw things, like the brick that an ACT UP Los Angeles member hurled through a window. Some protesters were arrested for shoving officers

FIGHT AIDS!

Members of the Tombstoners protest outside the Food and Drug Administration headquarters, October 1988.

who had first shoved them. By the end of the nine-hour protest, officers had made 185 arrests.

FIGHT AIDS

Although the protesters had not really seized control of the FDA building, they had captured the FDA's and the media's attention. The following day, the protest appeared in newspapers across the country, often on the first page. "1,000 Swarm FDA's Rockville Office to Demand Approval of AIDS Drugs," blasted the *Washington Post* headline.

Nine days after the protest, the FDA announced that it would change some of its rules governing the testing of experimental drugs. The purpose of the change was to evaluate and approve drugs as fast as they did with AZT.

Was the FDA finally bending?

Two events in the coming year suggested that the answer was yes. In May 1989, under intense pressure from ACT UP, the FDA approved the release of a drug that prevented blindness in PWAs. A month later, the FDA also approved the sale of aerosol pentamidine, a drug designed to prevent pneumocystis pneumonia (PCP) from occurring. PCP caused more deaths of PWAs than any other infection.

The approval of pentamidine was historic. It marked the first time that the FDA approved a drug based on a trial conducted by community-based physicians rather than by research scientists in federally funded labs. The San Francisco Community Consortium, organized by Dr. Donald Francis, had conducted its own trial of more than 400 PWAs, and the results from this grassroots work had provided the data for approval.

ACT UP and the consortium were delighted that the FDA was finally listening to patients and their doctors, but activists remained frustrated on other fronts. ACT UP New York member Jim Eigo was especially concerned about people with AIDS who were dying but had no access to the experimental drugs in NIH's clinical trials. Could he somehow change that?

33

DROPPING PRICES, EXCHANGING NEEDLES

JIM EIGO, A MEMBER OF ACT UP'S ISSUES COMMITTEE, FOCUSED ON ONE QUESTION: *How can we help dying PWAs access experimental drugs in government-sponsored trials?*

Clinical trials for experimental drugs had strict qualifications for participation, and thousands of dying PWAs were unqualified. Perhaps they didn't have the exact CD4 count—the number of a type of white blood cells—required by the test. Or perhaps they didn't have the right combination of symptoms.

Why don't we add another part to the trials? Eigo wondered.

The main part would follow the stringent rules of participation and continue to use placebos. Another part would accept unqualified PWAs who had no other reasonable treatment options. In effect, this second part would greatly expand access to experimental drugs.

Eigo pitched the idea to Anthony Fauci, and in June 1989, after months of meetings, Fauci publicly announced his support for what he called "the parallel track."

By the time other NIH and FDA leaders also backed it, the original idea had undergone significant revisions. But the primary goal was met.

Thousands of dying PWAs now had access to experimental drugs in the government's pipeline. It was a monumental victory.

But ACT UP did not stop to celebrate. Another vexing problem required a lot of attention—and a different type of action.

✊✊✊✊✊ ✊✊✊✊
F I G H T   A I D S

ACT UP New York was losing patience with Burroughs Wellcome, the company that manufactured AZT, the only drug approved to fight HIV.

The company was still charging an exorbitant price, and its profit margin—its income after its costs were subtracted from its revenue—had recently increased to 80 percent, an extraordinarily high number in the business world.

The high cost meant that PWAs without enough money to buy the drug were continuing to die. So ACT UP decided to hit the company in its most vulnerable spot—its stock price.

✊✊✊✊✊ ✊✊✊✊
F I G H T   A I D S

The New York Stock Exchange (NYSE) in Lower Manhattan was the place where Burroughs Wellcome stock was bought, sold, and traded. The value of the company rose and dove as the value of its stock did, and recent reports about the effectiveness of AZT had led to a 32 percent increase in the price of its stock.

ACT UP decided that, given the drug maker's concerns about its value, the NYSE would be the perfect place for the next protest.

On September 14, 1989, ACT UP member Peter Staley donned a business suit to disguise himself as a stockbroker. Six other ACT UP members, all dressed in suits, met him outside the NYSE. Everyone was wearing fake badges that would give them entry to the famous stock-trading floor.

The six activists blended into the crowd of stockbrokers spilling onto the floor. The fake badges did their trick—no one stopped them.

As the real stockbrokers checked the recent stock analyses, fielded calls, and watched the clock, waiting for the opening bell to ring at 9:30 a.m., four ACT UP members headed toward an unused balcony that overlooked the floor.

Upstairs, the four unpacked their bags and chained themselves to one another and a railing. Downstairs, the other two activists milled about on the floor, waiting to photograph the protest about to unfold.

Just before 9:30, the activists on the balcony speedily unfurled a banner that said, "Sell Wellcome." That was familiar stockbroker language telling the brokers to sell, or dump, their Burroughs Wellcome stock—an act that would plunge the value of the company.

Then the four blasted miniature airhorns across the trading floor. The sound was so loud, so obnoxious, so invasive, that the brokers turned their attention to the balcony rather than to the start of the business day. Looking up, they saw a shower of fake dollars with a pointed message: "We die while you make money. Fuck your profiteering."

The two ACT UP members on the floor snapped photos, dashed for the exits, and took off for the Associated Press office.

Security officers took off for the balcony. "DIE, FAGGOTS!" yelled the brokers. "MACE THEM!" It didn't take long to unchain the activists, or to haul them out of the NYSE, where a crowd of supporters cheered wildly as the police loaded them into a van.

Later in the day, about 1,500 ACT UP members stormed the streets around the NYSE, blowing whistles, blasting airhorns, and shouting, "Free AZT!"

Back in Washington, Anthony Fauci said, "The best way to get prices down is to get more drugs on the market and allow market forces to work."

But four days after the ACT UP protests, facing a barrage of critical articles in the national and international press, Burroughs Wellcome dropped the price of AZT by 20 percent. T+D member Mark Harrington described the cut as "a pretty strong indication that the company has been profiteering all along."

FIGHT AIDS

Together with protests targeting the FDA and Burroughs Wellcome, ACT UP was also taking direct action—and breaking the law—to address AIDS among people who injected drugs (PIDs).

On most Saturday mornings beginning in early 1990, ACT UP members joined Jon C. Parker, of the National AIDS Brigade, in a covert program in New York City that exchanged clean needles for dirty ones. The purpose of the program was not to promote drug use but to prevent the spread of HIV.

When the activists showed up in an area known for drug use, PIDs quickly lined up to exchange their needles. "Sometimes I feel like I'm in a park with breadcrumbs and all the pigeons come out of nowhere," Parker said.

Some PIDs had one needle to exchange, some had several, and some had ten and more. All of them knew that using dirty needles could result in contracting HIV, and all of them wanted to avoid HIV and AIDS.

"Jon's saved a lot of us," said one PID.

On March 6, 1990, Parker and ACT UP members set up a black card table displaying new syringes at the corner of Essex and Delancey Streets in Lower Manhattan. The table also had condoms and bleach for cleaning used needles.

Before the group of eight could exchange even one needle, police arrested them for illegal possession of hypodermic needles.

"We're trying to save lives," Parker protested.

It didn't matter—the law was the law—and all eight were hauled to jail.

While street activists continued to find a way to exchange needles, Mark Harrington was working his way through stacks of papers. Bleary eyed, he was beginning to ask questions that would eventually crack open the secret operations of the National Institutes of Health.

34

STORM THE NIH!

ACT UP MEMBER MARK HARRINGTON WAS PUZZLED ABOUT DRUG TRIALS AT THE National Institutes of Health (NIH). *Why was the NIH conducting so many studies of AZT?* he wondered. Why were 80 percent of trial volunteers channeled into AZT-related tests? Eighty percent!

And why were only 17 percent of volunteers in tests of drugs for opportunistic infections? Most PWAs die of these!

Harrington discovered that a group of five scientists decided on how to spend the NIH money designated for AIDS drug trials, and that in prior years, the five had served as paid research consultants to Burroughs Wellcome, the company that now manufactured AZT.

Was the company still paying the group of five? Were they favoring AZT studies because they made money from the company that manufactured AZT? Was the decision-making system corrupt?

Harrington asked the NIH for information about financial arrangements that might exist between the group of five and Burroughs Wellcome. The agency refused to divulge anything.

But the investigation into NIH's decision-making had clearly touched a nerve, and the agency soon responded by creating a Patient Constituency Working Group. The new group would consist of community physicians, PWAs, and AIDS activists, and they would be allowed to offer input into NIH's decision-making.

The move fulfilled one of ACT UP's longtime goals—to get people with HIV and AIDS at the decision-making table. But in what appeared to be a deliberate move to keep its most vocal critics out of the group, the NIH did not invite Harrington or ACT UP to join.

Rather than accepting defeat, Harrington convinced the new group to elect him as a member. But membership proved unhelpful, because the agency would not permit group members to attend crucial conference meetings that helped to decide which drugs would be tested.

In response, Harrington and the T+D committee developed a list of demands to give the agency:

> Open all decision-making meetings to the Patient Constituency Working Group.
> No more secrets!
> Cut financial ties between NIH-related scientists and drug companies.
> No more corruption!
> Start focusing on drugs to treat opportunistic infections.
> No more obsession with AZT!
> Increase enrollments of people of color, women, and children in drug trials.
> No more "medical apartheid"!

When the T+D committee outlined all the problems they faced with the NIH to the ACT UP membership, the response was quick and furious: *We need to seize control of the NIH!*

On the morning of May 21, 1990, about 1,200 ACT UP members from twenty states marched on NIH's headquarters in Bethesda,

Maryland. It was an historic moment—no one had ever marched on the NIH before.

Heading to the main administration building, several protesters carried long poles topped with unlit smoke bombs. Hundreds more carried flame-shaped signs saying, "We're Fired Up!"

"Act up! Fight back! Fight AIDS!" the marchers chanted. They also shouted out their anger about the NIH's focus on AZT: "Ten years, a billion dollars, one drug, big deal!"

Outside the building, protesters lit the yellow, green, purple, and red smoke bombs. Nearby, activists set up a mock graveyard and held a die-in. Dressed in all black, the Grim Reaper walked among tombstones that said, "AZT Is Not a Cure" and "One AIDS Death Every 12 Minutes." Every twelve minutes, activists blasted air horns.

The arrests began around 8:45 a.m. when Peter Staley climbed onto an overhang near the main building's entrance. He was quickly subdued, handcuffed, and taken to a police van. As fast as he had been arrested, activists surrounded the van and sat down.

A group of sit-inners blocking the building's side entrance were also arrested and hauled away. So were twenty-one activists who managed to hold a sit-in at the office of Daniel Hoth, the director of clinical trials for AIDS drugs.

At the same time, different ACT UP groups staged protests for women, people of color, and impoverished people. Women activists built an "invisible" house for women with AIDS who were denied access to drug trials. Wrapped in medical gauze, they chanted, "NIH, your name's a lie! You test mice while women die!" A big black banner read, "NIH: Wake Up and Smell the Women."

In another area, a defiant Black protester with a bullhorn said, "This is a story about racism. This is a story about sexism. This is a story about greed. And this is war! There are people of color, women,

ACT UP protest at the National Institutes of Health in Bethesda, Maryland, May 1990.

IV-drug users, children, Latinos, Latinas, Asians . . . dying for AIDS treatment." Black protesters in black T-shirts that said "Death" led a loud chant: "People of color are under attack! What do we do? We fight back!"

Black activist Phyllis Sharpe, an HIV-positive mother with an HIV-positive daughter, represented impoverished PWAs. "I have a home now, but ten months ago I was still homeless," she said. "Many people who are here today are still homeless right now. One thing I can tell you about the NIH—they don't have any homeless people in their trials, and they don't have trials for drug users."

The national media—radio, television, and newspapers—reported on the protest, and the *Washington Post* published Anthony Fauci's reaction. "It was interesting theater, but it was not helpful."

But no one in the media reported on the most significant criticism leveled during the protest. It happened when T+D member Garance Franke-Ruta, wearing a white lab coat, pointed at the NIH building and blasted it for not focusing on "protease inhibitors," experimental drugs that seemed to have the ability to stop HIV from spreading. *Why wasn't the NIH pouring its resources into studying protease inhibitors?*

History would show that Franke-Ruta was asking the right question, but that the NIH wasn't ready to listen.

35

WINS AND LOSSES

ACT UP NEW YORK DEBATED AND CLASHED AND CLASHED AND DEBATED.

About 100 AIDS organizations were planning to boycott the Sixth International AIDS Conference, scheduled for June 1990 in San Francisco, to express opposition to a government policy prohibiting HIV-infected travelers from entering the United States. But T+D activists opposed the boycott because the conference, with 950 delegates from 121 countries, promised to be a treasure trove of information about recent developments in AIDS research.

Plus, conference chair John Ziegler had even *invited* T+D member Peter Staley to speak at the opening session. It seemed like the scientific community was finally offering an olive branch to the activist community.

After intense debate, ACT UP adopted an inside-outside strategy for the conference. Some activists would protest outside the conference, and some would seek to gain valuable information, while still vocalizing their objections, inside the conference.

On the afternoon of June 20, about 500 AIDS activists protested outside the Moscone Center, where opening ceremonies would begin at 4:00 p.m. They marched with protest signs. They burned a US flag. And they held a mock trial, with a judge and jury, charging NIH-affiliated researchers with failing to make AIDS drugs more accessible and affordable. "Guilty! Guilty! Guilty!"

Inside, John Ziegler opened the conference with a plea for mutual respect between activists and scientists. But he wasn't sure the plea would work, especially when Staley, dressed in a black shirt and wearing an ACT UP button, walked toward the speaker's podium. *Would he unleash ACT UP on them?*

The question became even more urgent when Staley asked AIDS activists in the audience to gather in front of the stage. About 300 activists stood up from their seats and poured to the front.

Staley then issued an invitation to the entire audience: "If you believe that the present INS [Immigration and Naturalization Service] barring people living with HIV disease from entering this country is useless as health policy and discriminatory as well, please stand now and remain standing."

Remarkably, virtually all audience members stood and applauded. They even joined the AIDS activists in chanting, "Change the law!" After another chant, a smiling Staley invited them to return to their seats. "You can all now consider yourselves members of ACT UP," he said.

For the bulk of his speech, Staley lamented the sharp clashes between scientists and activists. "Can we all, before it's too late, begin to understand each other?" he asked. "Will we realize that we share similar motivations? Can we try, at least this week, to bridge the widening gap between us?"

For the most part, ACT UP honored the conference's request that they not "obstruct the flow of information." But the activists announced that they would not abide by the request when Louis W. Sullivan, the secretary of Health and Human Services in the new administration of President George H. W. Bush, spoke at the closing session.

In a flyer explaining their upcoming protest, ACT UP said: "After 10 years of Bush/Reagan rhetoric on AIDS, we will no longer tolerate words without action."

About 500 AIDS activists stormed the stage when Secretary Sullivan was introduced. They unfurled a pink banner that read, "He Talks, We Die." They blasted air horns. They blew whistles. They chanted, "We die! They do nothing!" During the secretary's speech, they threw condoms onto the stage.

Yes, ACT UP would collaborate with scientists, but when face-to-face with a presidential administration that they saw as discriminating against people with HIV, ACT UP returned to its core—loud, direct, and confrontational.

After the conference, Mark Harrington declared victory in an article he penned for the magazine *OutWeek*. The scientific AIDS community had finally admitted AIDS activists "into the system," he wrote.

Victories were everywhere. Secret meetings at the NIH were disappearing. Members of the Patient Constituency Working Group were gaining voting privileges on all committees.

The NIH was placing more emphasis on studying opportunistic infections and women with HIV. And the agency was now requiring scientists to disclose any financial arrangements they had with drug companies.

"None of this could have happened without the efforts of thousands of people with AIDS over the last

Protest with air horns at the closing session of the Sixth International AIDS conference in San Francisco, June 1990.

ten years and those of the hundreds of activists who stormed the NIH on May 21," Harrington concluded.

The article left some women activists fuming, and they responded with a flurry of letters to the editor. Heidi Dorow of ACT UP New York took issue with Harrington's claim about new access. "We don't have access or input," she said. "What we have is women dying six times faster than men. We are ten years into this epidemic, and we still have no clue as to how many women have HIV, how it will manifest itself in their bodies, or how to treat it in those women's bodies."

Tracey Morgan, also of ACT UP New York, wrote that she saw little difference between Harrington and "the boys" at NIH. "From your article, my fear is that you have sacrificed women," she wrote. "The sisterhood is watching, brother. Don't fuck us over."

The women's criticism revealed a growing division within ACT UP. The inside-outside strategy was reaching a breaking point.

Women leaders, as well as others, were increasingly concerned that Harrington and the T+D committee were growing so close to the scientific community that they were losing their critical edge. And Harrington and the T+D committee were increasingly disturbed with activists who seemed content to remain on the outside of important meetings about getting drugs into bodies. For Harrington and his friends, protest alone was ineffective.

In November 1991, T+D split from ACT UP and renamed itself. The new Treatment Action Group would seek to reform the scientific AIDS community from within, which it believed could do a better job of solving the AIDS crisis.

Unfazed, ACT UP New York labored on, continuing to emphasize protests as an effective method for forcing politicians and scientists to confront the AIDS crisis *now*.

But T+D and ACT UP members weren't the only major activists in the fight against AIDS. Other organizations were wielding power, and they were about to score a massive victory that would improve AIDS care for decades to come.

PART NINE
CONGRESS AND THE COURTS, BROADWAY AND THE WHITE HOUSE

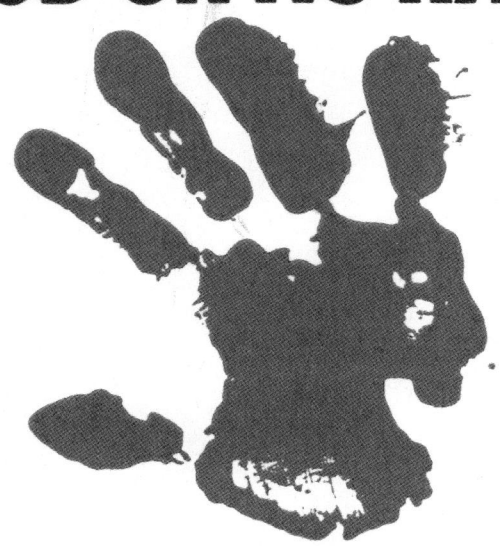

"BLOOD ON ITS HANDS." Poster and stickers created by artist group Gran Fury.

36

THE LEGACY OF RYAN WHITE

THOMAS SHERIDAN WAS AMAZED AS HE WALKED THROUGH WARD 5B AT SAN Francisco General Hospital.

The nation's first AIDS ward had changed a lot since first opening. Earlier, most patients were gay men, but now there were also drug users and women on the ward.

It felt like a "war zone," Sheridan said, but it was also "the most compassionate health care environment I've ever seen—doctors, nurses, volunteers, patients, friends, and family members were all in—one unit of love and care."

The visit introduced Sheridan to the type of AIDS care that could be supported and advanced across the country—if only Congress would pass an AIDS bill.

Back in Washington, DC, where he worked with a coalition of 120 organizations known as "the infamous AIDS lobby," Sheridan and his colleagues helped to craft a new bill focused on ensuring care for PWAs.

On March 6, 1990, Democratic Senator Ted Kennedy and Republican Senator Orrin Hatch introduced the bill in the Senate. The bill would provide $300 million in emergency assistance to cities facing the worst

AIDS problems. Another $300 million would fund grants targeting rural areas.

Actress Elizabeth Taylor—who had continued to work on behalf of AIDS patients since her friend Rock Hudson died and was the nation's best-known AIDS fundraiser—flew in from Los Angeles to testify at the bill's first public hearing. Her presence created a stir among the senators, and in the following weeks, she continued her lobbying efforts by sending letters on scented purple stationery.

FIGHT AIDS

Near the end of March, President George H. W. Bush delivered his first speech on AIDS since taking office fifteen months earlier. At the National Coalition on AIDS conference, the president announced his support for a bill that would prohibit discrimination against people with AIDS and other disabilities.

The president was keenly aware that critics of the bill scoffed at providing legal protections for gay men whose sexual behavior resulted in AIDS. *Why do we have to protect them? They did it to themselves!*

"We don't spurn the accident victim who didn't wear a seat belt," Bush countered. "We don't reject the cancer patient who didn't quit smoking cigarettes. We try to love them and care for them and comfort them. We do not fire them. We don't evict them. We don't cancel their insurance."

LGBTQ legal groups, like Lambda Legal, had long used the courts to fight discrimination, and AIDS lobbyists had long fought for an antidiscrimination law. But LGBTQ leaders didn't jump out of their seats and cheer the president. They wanted more—they wanted Bush to announce his support for the AIDS care bill sponsored by Senators Kennedy and Hatch.

The president did not publicly back the bill, and without his support, the bill stalled in the Senate. Then, horrible news struck: Ryan White was dying.

FIGHT AIDS

The pop singer and songwriter Elton John was at Ryan's bedside at Riley Hospital for Children in Indianapolis when Senator Kennedy called. *Ryan's in a coma,* John told the senator. Ryan had a severe case of pneumocystis pneumonia, and the only thing keeping him alive was a respirator.

Kennedy shared the news with those working on the AIDS bill, and Senator Hatch suggested they name the bill after Ryan. The two senators soon spoke with Ryan's mother, Jeanne, and asked her permission to name the bill in honor of Ryan. "Well, I'm not sure what to say," Jeanne replied. "I mean, I guess that would be great. Ryan would be honored—*we* would be honored."

The senators thanked Jeanne for being so generous at such a devastating moment in her life. The new bill would be called the Ryan White Comprehensive AIDS Resources Emergency (CARE) Act.

On April 8, 1990, Ryan White died. He was only eighteen years old. About 1,500 people, including Elton John and First Lady Barbara Bush, attended his funeral.

FIGHT AIDS

Just one week later, Tom Sheridan of the AIDS lobby called Jeanne with an urgent request. "Jeanne," he said, "I know this is a difficult time . . . and I'm not sure how to even ask this . . . but we need you here in Washington. We don't have the support we need yet for the CARE bill, for Ryan's bill, and I need you to come and talk to some senators here."

Two days later, Jeanne was inside the US Capitol, talking with senators about Ryan and the need for a new AIDS care law. A short while into the conversation, about seventy-five friends and family members of other people who had died of AIDS joined her. They had been enlisted by the Gay Men's Health Crisis—the main organization that provided care to PWAs in New York City.

ACT UP, with its focus on drug treatment, did not carry out any protests in support of the CARE bill. But Tom Sheridan used ACT UP's militant actions to build support among senators. As he explained it, "Every time ACT UP pulled something new, I tried to use the opportunity to remind members of Congress that unless I could work with them to produce some modicum of progress on AIDS policy, actions like this were likely to persist."

Most members of Congress, according to Sheridan, were "turned off" by ACT UP's militancy—but also by the unbending stance of far-right politicians who shut down any attempt to pass a law that provided care for PWAs. "The crazier the crazies became," Sheridan said, "the more members wished to be associated with a moderate middle ground"—the ground that the CARE bill offered them.

On August 4, 1990, the House and the Senate passed the final version of the Ryan White CARE Act. One hurdle remained: President Bush.

A week earlier, the president had signed the Americans with Disabilities Act (ADA) of 1990, delivering a massive victory to PWAs, AIDS activists, and AIDS lobbyists. The act defined PWAs as disabled, outlawed discrimination against them in jobs and housing, and expanded their access to public accommodations.

But it was not clear that the president would sign the Ryan

White CARE Act. Unlike the ADA—which covered all people with disabilities—the CARE Act focused only on PWAs. Plus, the president generally opposed increases to the federal budget, and the CARE Act would eventually commit the federal government to spending hundreds of millions of dollars.

So AIDS lobbyist Tom Sheridan called President Bush's chief counsel with a threat: "Should the president choose to veto or threaten to veto the bill, ACT UP would join forces with Jeanne White and all of the mothers who'd come to the Senate, and they'd meet at the front gates of the White House to express their outrage."

On August 18, 1990, President Bush signed the Ryan White CARE Act into law. He did not invite Jeanne White or any PWAs to come to the White House for a public signing of the bill. Instead, without any fanfare, he signed the legislation on a plane trip to Los Angeles.

The Ryan White CARE Act had just become the largest federally funded program for PWAs, supporting and expanding the medical care and social services they so desperately needed.

Still, not everyone received the care they required. Impoverished PWAs were especially vulnerable to insufficient care, and no one knew this better than Katrina Haslip.

37

WOMEN, POOR PEOPLE, AND DISCRIMINATION

KATRINA HASLIP LEARNED THAT SHE WAS HIV-POSITIVE WHEN SHE WAS SERVING TIME at Bedford Hills Correctional Facility in New York.

It did not take long for her to discover that services for women prisoners with HIV and AIDS were abysmal. "Women were dying in their cells and in the hospitals," she said. "They were dying because they were giving up and because there was no hope."

Haslip also saw that inmates and security guards kept their distance from her and other infected women. Like many others, they thought they might contract AIDS through casual contact.

Haslip cofounded the prison's AIDS Counseling and Education Program. The counseling wing helped women prisoners talk openly about their diagnosis, and the education wing taught the prison community about HIV, AIDS, and the facts of transmission.

HIV-positive women turned to Haslip with all kinds of questions, including legal ones, and sometimes she referred them to lawyer Theresa McGovern, an advocate for poor people in New York City.

FIGHT AIDS

After her release from prison in September 1990, Haslip helped formerly incarcerated HIV-positive women readapt to society. Most of the women were poor, and they desperately needed federal benefits to access health care, food, and shelter. Again, Haslip referred them to McGovern.

McGovern saw impoverished women with AIDS on a regular basis, and she used the legal system to advocate for them as well as for other people with AIDS, including drug users and people without homes. The main challenge she noticed was that the Social Security Administration (SSA)—which oversaw federal benefits for people with AIDS—required applicants to meet the government's definition of AIDS as a condition for receiving benefits. If an applicant's illnesses did not match the definition provided by the CDC, they could not receive financial assistance.

Many of McGovern's clients were suffering from vaginal infections, bacterial pneumonia (which is different from pneumocystis pneumonia), tuberculosis, and kidney failure, but, according to the CDC's definition, these disabling conditions were not complications of AIDS.

Frustrated, McGovern believed that the government's definition was far too limited. She also discovered that it was based on the CDC's early studies of middle-class gay men. The definition did not consider the way that AIDS manifested itself in women or poor people.

So, on October 1, 1990, McGovern filed a lawsuit against the Social Security Administration, claiming that it wrongly denied benefits because it used an inaccurate and outdated definition. The plaintiffs in the lawsuit included Haslip and a group of the women she had referred to McGovern.

ACT UP New York scheduled a protest to draw attention to the lawsuit. One day after the filing, about 200 AIDS activists, including McGovern and her plaintiffs, gathered outside the Health and Human Services (HHS) building in Washington, DC. HHS was the federal agency that oversaw both the CDC and the SSA.

The activists marched in an elongated circle in front of the building. "How many women have to die before you say we qualify?" they chanted.

While some conducted a die-in, others held fluorescent pink foamboards cut into the shape of tombstones. Their messages said that women with HIV get pelvic inflammatory diseases, vaginal candidiasis, pulmonary tuberculosis, and liver disease—and yet none of these were part of the CDC definition. "Women are dying for AIDS treatment," a sign said.

Protesting the failure of government agencies to define and address the impact of AIDS on women, outside the department of Health and Human Services in Washington, DC, October 1990.

Plaintiffs in the lawsuit also shared personal stories about their inability to receive federal benefits. Phyllis Sharpe said that although she suffered from urinary tract infections, chronic diarrhea, and shortness of breath, the SSA refused to classify her as a PWA. Iris de la Cruz—a thirty-eight-year-old woman with AIDS, added, "One of the reasons why women remain untreated is because they don't have Medicaid, and they have no access to health care."

When asked to comment on the protest, Social Security Commissioner Gwendolyn King sounded sympathetic. "We recognize our responsibility to continue to revise our procedures, seek broader flexibility, improve our guidelines and instructions to ensure that we . . . eliminate all artificial barriers" to federal benefits.

But activists did not detect any improvements in the following month, so they decided to head directly to the CDC. They had held a protest there back in January, but this one was bigger and bolder.

It was pouring rain on December 3, 1990, when 500 people marched from a nearby street to the CDC headquarters in Atlanta, shouting out chants tailor-made for the occasion: "CDC, it's a disaster! Women die faster!" "Murder by omission! Change the definition!"

Several activists chained themselves to the doors, and others stormed the building, even gaining access to the director's office. The arrests came fast. As police officers dragged a protester away, she shouted, "They do nothing! Women die!" By the end of the day, about 100 people had been arrested.

A CDC spokesperson said that while its scientists were "continuing to look at this whole spectrum of AIDS in women including these gynecological conditions," they currently lacked the data required to update the definition. "We may at some point expand our case definition, but we're not ready to do that at this point," he said.

A few weeks later, scientists at the first National Conference on Women and HIV Infection joined the criticism. About a dozen studies showed that some women with HIV suffered from cervical cancer and other illnesses not included in the CDC's definition. "Errors of omission are matters of life and death," said Dr. Judith Hoven, an AIDS expert from San Francisco General Hospital.

Data from California added to the troubling news. The statistics indicated that women with AIDS died faster than men with AIDS. The average survival time for women was seven months; the average time for men was two years. Women were also more likely than men to die within a month after receiving their diagnosis.

The conference laid out other disturbing statistics:

> About 15,000 women had met the government's criteria for AIDS; another 100,000 were HIV-positive.
>
> AIDS in US men was increasing by 18 percent a year; AIDS in women was increasing by 29 percent a year.
>
> The death rate for Black women with AIDS was *nine times higher* than the death rate for White women with AIDS.
>
> Women constituted only 10 percent of those enrolled in federal AIDS studies.

NIH AIDS director Daniel Hoth and Anthony Fauci did not deny that they and others had neglected to study women with AIDS.

"Frankly, I can say very little about the treatment of AIDS in women," Hoth conceded. "I stand before you, stating: We simply haven't done

ACT UP poster demanding research into the impact of AIDS on women.

enough. It certainly wasn't intentional. But what is important is the future. We will do everything we can to get answers to the questions women and their doctors need to know."

Fauci added that the National Institute of Allergy and Infectious Diseases would undertake a large and long-term study of women with AIDS. But neither he nor Hoth advocated for expanding the CDC's definition of AIDS.

38

WEARING RED RIBBONS

AIDS WAS DEVASTATING THE ARTISTIC COMMUNITY IN NEW YORK.

"The East Village art scene felt like it was disappearing overnight because of AIDS," photographer Allen Frame recalled.

The wreckage left surviving artists with a burning desire to create something positive. "We had no choice," Frame said. "We had to do something with our professional lives."

So in the spring of 1991, fifteen artists and art professionals met at a shared gallery space to brainstorm about what they could do. They called themselves the Visual AIDS Artists Caucus, and they quickly agreed on the need to create a symbol to raise awareness about AIDS, honor those who had died, and express solidarity with the living.

Painter Frank Moore suggested a ribbon project of some sort. Around the country, millions of yellow ribbons were on display to show support for US soldiers serving in the Persian Gulf. Moore thought that Visual AIDS might somehow adapt the idea for the cause of AIDS.

Within a couple hours, the group decided to create a small ribbon that people could wear on shirts and jackets, pants and bags, and hats and running shoes.

A simple ribbon. And "self-replicating," as cofounder Patrick

O'Connell put it. "You cut the ribbon 6–7 inches, loop it around your finger, and pin it on. You can do it yourself."

Next up was the question of color. The group ruled out pink and rainbow colors because they were so closely tied to the LGBTQ community. AIDS was not a gay disease.

What about red? The organization Mothers Against Drunk Driving gave out about 100 million red ribbons a year, so there was a possibility of confusing their campaign with an AIDS one. But the artists settled on red anyway. "Largely for symbolic reasons," Frank Moore said. "The connection to blood and the idea of passion—not only anger but love, like a valentine."

Plus, red was "vibrant and attention-getting," O'Connell said.

Now, how to share it as widely as possible? The group reached out to Rodger McFarlane, the activist who had started the helpline at the Gay Men's Health Crisis, and Tom Viola. Both men were now leading the Broadway theater industry's efforts to fight AIDS, and they agreed to distribute the ribbons at the upcoming, and nationally televised, Tony Awards.

Visual AIDS soon hosted a ribbon-making bee, where they made about 3,000 ribbons in about five hours, and then whisked them to the Miskoff Theater on Broadway, where the awards ceremony would be held.

During the ceremony, actor Jeremy Irons wore the ribbon on his lapel as he walked onstage. It was prominent, unmissable, and Visual AIDS members were amazed.

That simple act "snowballed," according to O'Connell, and within days, demands for the ribbon skyrocketed. Before long, groups across the country were hosting their own ribbon-making bees and raising awareness about AIDS in their local communities.

A Visual AIDS Red Ribbon Bee at the Clocktower, 1991.

The *New York Times* guessed that the symbol was so popular "because it was designed from the start to be inoffensive." An earlier effort to get celebrities to wear pins with an AIDS symbol had been unsuccessful. That symbol was the SILENCE = DEATH one designed by Avram Finkelstein and his friends.

ACT UP member Ann Northrop was critical of the red ribbon. "I wouldn't be surprised to see [President George H. W.] Bush himself wear one someday—that's how banal it's become," she said. "The element that is missing in the ribbons is anger. People can be sympathetic from here to sunset but that won't stop a quarantine."

Those who created and supported the ribbon also recognized its limitations. "I never want this to seem like anything more than visibility," said Rodger McFarlane. "The ribbon does not feed people or protect them from discrimination or provide leadership or a cure. But it is, at least, an easy first step."

It was a step easily taken by millions of everyday people whose personality was unlike ACT UP's and yet who wanted to express their solidarity with PWAs and the movement against AIDS.

The red ribbon wasn't a cure, but it became the most recognizable symbol in the history of the fight against AIDS.

39

ASHES FOR THE WHITE HOUSE

RACHEL PEPPER, A WRITER BASED IN THE SAN FRANCISCO BAY AREA, WAS AWESTRUCK as she listened to David Wojnarowicz (pronounced voy-nah-ROH-vitch). Her hero was giving a public reading of *Close to the Knives*, his fiery memoir about living and dying with AIDS.

"Although he was obviously sick, he projected more life from him that one hour than most people display in a lifetime," Pepper later wrote.

Wojnarowicz's rage-filled book captivated lots of people who were active in the fight against AIDS. Back in New York, a small ACT UP group called the Marys focused on his provocative words about AIDS deaths and protests:

> I imagine what it would be like if, each time a lover, friend or stranger died of this disease, their friends, lovers or neighbors would take the dead body and drive with it in a car a hundred miles an hour to washington d.c. and blast through the gates of the white house and come to a screeching halt before the entrance and dump their lifeless form on the front steps.

The Marys were inspired. According to Joy Episalla, "we started thinking—goddamn right, that sounds just about right to us. So we decided that that's what we were going to do."

Their plan was to talk with PWAs to see if they might be interested in agreeing to a political funeral, a public event where their friends would use their death, and perhaps their ashes or corpse, to draw attention to the government's failures in the AIDS crisis.

Meanwhile, ACT UP San Francisco member David Robinson decided to mail the ashes of his late partner, Warren, to President George H. W. Bush, along with a protest letter that partly faulted him for Warren's death. But a few friends convinced him to make his protest more public, more visible, and to invite others to become part of it.

Robinson agreed, and he enlisted support from ACT UP organizations across the United States. Together, they would meet in Washington, march to the White House, and dump the ashes of their late friends and partners on the lawn.

On October 11, 1992, the AIDS Quilt was back on display in Washington, DC. That day, about 2,000 AIDS activists marched down the National Mall and past the quilt.

"I think the Quilt itself does beautiful things, and is moving," Robinson said. "Still, it's like making something beautiful out of the epidemic. And I felt like doing something like this [the ashes march] is a way of showing there's nothing beautiful about it. This is what I'm left with—I've got a box full of ashes and bone chips. There's no beauty in that."

Fifteen people carrying ashes in plastic bags, boxes, and urns led the march, their faces showing anguish and resolve. Sometimes the 2,000 activists were quiet, marching to the slow beat of the drums and holding protest signs and photos of their loved ones. Other times, they chanted angrily: "Bringing the ashes to your door! We won't take it anymore!" "150,000 dead! Where was George?"

Several marchers carried posters showing the White House with bloody handprints on either side. Its message said, "11 Years of Neglect of the AIDS Crisis. White House = Death House."

Before arriving at the White House, David Robinson addressed the crowd. "We're showing everyone . . . the actual results of what that White House, this administration, has done. They have turned the people we love into ashes and bone chips and corpses. That should not be hidden. . . . We're not going to hide this anymore, because hiding is what they want."

Police officers on horses awaited the march's arrival at the White House gate. As the marchers drew close, those who were willing to be arrested joined hands and formed a barrier between the officers and those with ashes. The rest of the crowd shouted, "Act up! Fight back! Fight AIDS!"

Robinson grabbed the top of the White House fence with his left hand and climbed part of the way up. Steadying himself, he uncovered his small gold box, took out a plastic bag holding Warren's ashes and bone chips, dumped them across the lush green lawn, and pitched the box toward the White House.

Turning from the fence, he saw two close friends with tears streaming down their cheeks. Robinson grabbed both men and held them tight.

Close by, a mother who had just scattered her son's ashes pumped her arms. "Yesss!" she said.

One marcher called to mind his grandmother—a Black woman in the South. She had surprised him by giving her stamp of approval for today's protest. In the days of lynching, she said, Black people retrieved the hanging rope and burned it to ashes.

As the dumping of the ashes concluded, the crowd was no longer

ACT UP protestors throw ashes onto the White House lawn, 1992.

somber. They cheered and whistled and screamed and shouted. "Act up! Fight back! Fight AIDS!" Walking away, they clasped one another's hands and held them high.

FIGHT AIDS

President Bush did not witness the protest. He had already left for that evening's presidential election debate, where he squared off against Governor Bill Clinton and billionaire businessman Ross Perot.

During the debate, Bush complained about Magic Johnson, the HIV-positive basketball star, resigning from the National Commission on AIDS. In late September, Johnson had quit, saying the president had "dropped the ball on AIDS." He meant that President Bush had rejected or declined all the panel's recommendations.

Rather than using the debate to address Johnson's specific concerns, Bush lauded the funds that his administration had earmarked for the AIDS fight and commended First Lady Barbara Bush—who had been photographed holding a baby with AIDS—for breaking down the stigma of AIDS. He also criticized ACT UP as "extreme."

"Do not go to the extreme," the president warned the country.

ACT UP did not heed the warning.

40

VICTORIES DESPITE DEATH

ON OCTOBER 29, 1992, MARK LOWE FISHER DIED OF AIDS. HE WAS THIRTY-NINE years old.

Four days later, his friends gathered for his funeral at Judson Memorial Church in Greenwich Village. At the front of the church was Fisher's partially open casket. He was wearing the black ACT UP T-shirt that he had worn to so many protests.

His friends paused to pay their respects. Some stood at arm's length, but others touched his cheeks, stroked his arms, and kissed his forehead.

Fisher had been part of the Marys, the ACT UP group committed to holding political funerals, and Mary member Joy Episalla read aloud an article in which he had described his funeral wishes.

"I want to show the reality of my death, to display my body in public; I want the public to bear witness. We are not just spiraling statistics; we are people who have purpose, who have lovers, friends, and families. . . . I want my own funeral to be fierce and defiant, to make the public statement that my death from AIDS is a form of political assassination."

At the end of the service, Fisher's friends lifted his casket—it was still partially open—and walked out the front of the church. Rain drops fell on the corpse before umbrellas covered it for the evening procession.

Leading the way was a black banner: "Mark Lowe Fisher, 1953–1992, Died of AIDS, Murdered By George Bush." More than 200 people followed, their chants angry and unrelenting. "George Bush, you can't hide! We charge you with genocide!" "Mark Fisher died from AIDS! Where was George?" "Bush did nothing! Mark died!"

The thirty-five-block procession stopped outside President Bush's campaign headquarters in Midtown Manhattan, and several ACT UP members offered stinging comments.

"It was Mark's wish that we deliver his body to the doorstep of the man who murdered him," one said. "George Bush, we charge you with the murder of Mark Fisher and with the genocide of millions of

Funeral and protest for Mark Fisher, New York, October 1992.

people with HIV. George Bush, you killed Mark Fisher through your murderous neglect."

As always, ACT UP responded: "Act up! Fight back! Fight AIDS!"

The following day, President Bush lost his bid for reelection. The new president would be former Arkansas governor Bill Clinton, whose campaign had promised the appointment of an AIDS "czar" to lead a national campaign, the acceleration of approval for AIDS drugs, robust funding for the Ryan White CARE Act, the distribution of condoms in supportive public schools, and an end to discrimination against HIV-positive immigrants.

As Clinton prepared to enter the White House, Katrina Haslip—who had fought to expand the CDC's definition of AIDS—was fighting for her life at Roosevelt Hospital in New York City.

Bacterial pneumonia had filled her lungs and left her exhausted. Her voice was reduced to a whisper, and she rarely opened her eyes when speaking to the *New York Times* reporter at her bedside. "I am, and have been, a woman with AIDS despite the CDC not wishing to count me," she said.

The current CDC definition still did not list bacterial pneumonia as an indicator of AIDS. Nor did it list a low count of CD4 cells—the ones that help fight infections—as a reliable sign of AIDS. Haslip's was 6; the normal count was 500 and up.

But finally, the CDC was bending. The center was now proposing to expand its definition to include four new conditions: cervical cancer, pulmonary tuberculosis, bacterial pneumonia, and CD4 counts of 200 or less.

"We have compelled them," Haslip said.

She was right. The shift was the result of the sustained campaign carried out by Haslip, lawyer Theresa McGovern, ACT UP, other AIDS organizations, doctors, and HIV-positive patients excluded from the definition.

But Haslip, ever the fighter, wasn't completely satisfied with the expanded definition. She was disturbed that it didn't include other conditions common in women with HIV—for example, pelvic inflammation and vaginal yeast infections.

As she lay dying, Haslip also recalled the horrible effects of the earlier definition. "So many women have died before they [the CDC] listened," she said.

On December 2, 1992, Katrina Haslip died. She was only thirty-three years old.

At the time of her death, the CDC's expanded definition still had not been approved. But a month later, it finally became official. Immediately, the number of people with AIDS virtually doubled, with women, children, IV drug users, people of color, and impoverished people comprising the majority of additions.

Several months later, the Social Security Administration began to distribute federal benefits using the expanded definition. The new policy gave thousands upon thousands of PWAs the financial assurances that Katrina Haslip never had.

More good news for women with AIDS arrived in early 1993 when Congress approved a bill reauthorizing the National Institutes of Health. The bill—which the Treatment Action Group and other AIDS groups had helped to write—required the NIH to include and expand the involvement of women in all research.

But, as so often happens, bad news appeared on the horizon.

PART TEN
FROM BLEAKNESS TO BREAKTHROUGH

FIGHT AIDS

DEMAND AN AIDS CURE NOW!

"DEMAND AN AIDS CURE NOW."
Poster by ACT UP, 1992.

41

ONE OF THE BLEAKEST MOMENTS

PRESIDENT CLINTON WAS BOGGED DOWN IN A BATTLE TO ALLOW GAY MEN AND lesbian women to serve openly in the military, and he was neglecting the AIDS promises he had made during his campaign.

AIDS activists were livid. They had been expecting the immediate appointment of an AIDS "czar": Someone with the power to create and manage a national campaign. Someone who would secure all the funds required for AIDS care. And demand that schools teach ways to prevent HIV. And deliver effective drugs to bodies.

Clinton did not appoint an AIDS czar. But in June 1993, six months after entering the Oval Office, he finally named Kristine Gebbie, a former nurse with experience on AIDS commissions, as the national AIDS policy coordinator.

Gebbie saw her job as building consensus among the federal agencies working on AIDS, and as coordinating their various efforts. She did not see herself as an AIDS czar. In fact, the president had not given her the power or authority required to direct a national campaign.

FIGHT AIDS

Two days after Gebbie's appointment, the *New York Times* published a shocking article about AZT. The early hopes for AZT had not been borne out by a longer study with a larger group of patients. A new AIDS study in Europe had just shown that the drug did not slow the rate of progression from HIV to AIDS. Nor did it prolong the life of a person with AIDS.

Reporter Lawrence K. Altman, who was not given to hyperbole, wrote, "It is one of the bleakest moments in the fight against the disease since AIDS was first recognized as a new disease in 1981."

The news fueled a sense of hopelessness among scientists, activists, and people with HIV and AIDS. Peter Staley of the Treatment Action Group admitted defeat. The strategy of pushing hard for fast cures or near-cures, and reforming the National Institutes of Health, had not resulted in an effective AIDS drug.

By this point, about 200,000 US citizens had died of AIDS, and the number was climbing fast. What was left to do other than to cry out in anguish?

On July 1, 1993, just two days after Altman's article, Joy Episalla escorted the corpse of her late friend, Tim Bailey, to Washington, DC.

By the time her van pulled into a parking lot near the US Capitol, two busloads of ACT UP New York members had already arrived. The plan was to hold a funeral procession from there to the White House. But there was a major glitch: Police officers refused to let ACT UP remove Bailey's body from the van.

Jamie Bauer—ACT UP's expert in civil disobedience—told the officers they were acting improperly. "This is a nonviolent political funeral procession for Tim Bailey," she explained. "This is not a demonstration.

ONE OF THE BLEAKEST MOMENTS

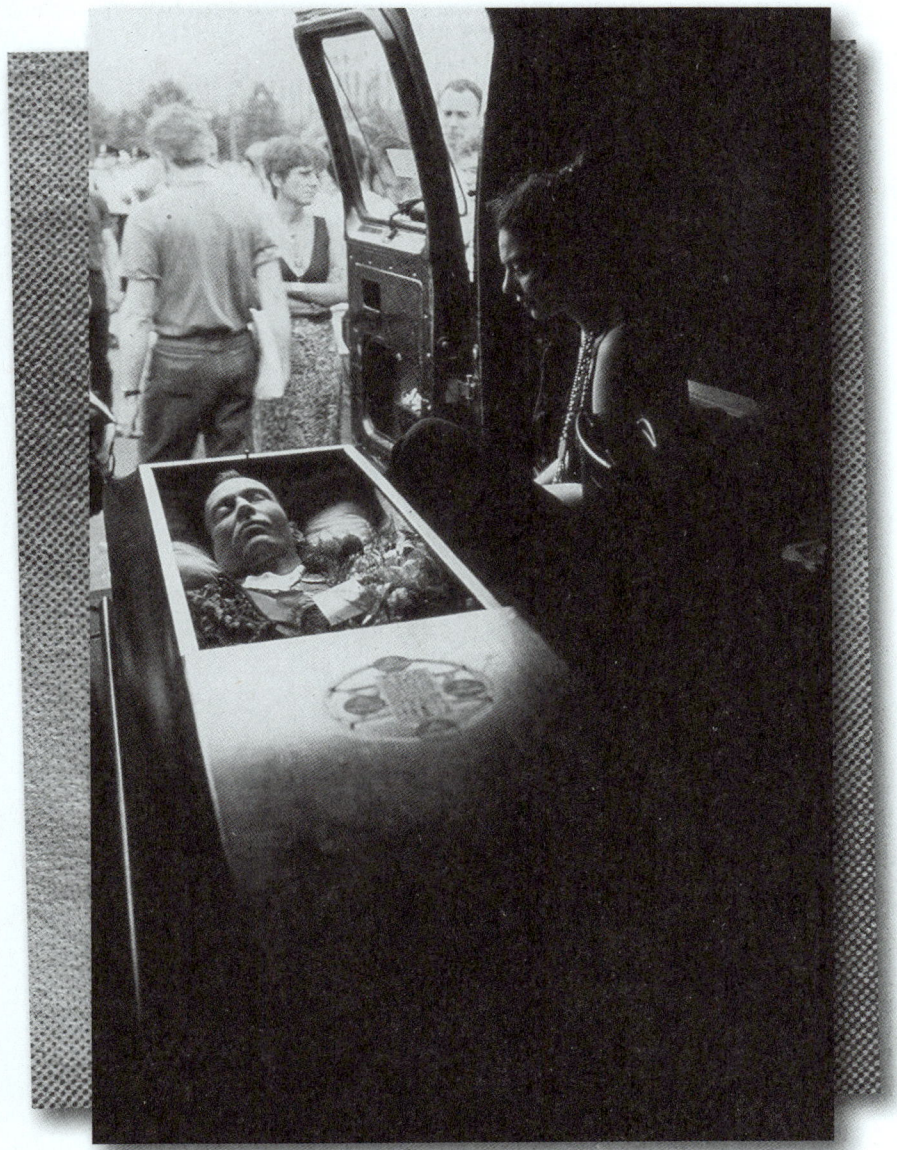

Tim Bailey, Washington, DC, July 1993.

This is a procession. We are going to proceed with this coffin to the White House as a funeral procession. We're not breaking any laws."

The officers were not convinced, and Joy Episalla lost her patience. "There is nothing that we would let happen to Tim," she yelled at the officers. "Actually, there's nothing you could do that could be worse than what he's fucking gone through in the last fucking year!"

The standoff erupted into chaos when ACT UP members forced their way to the casket and began to pull it out of the van. The partially open casket, which revealed Tim's face and shoulders, went up and down and sideways. Piercing screams added to the horror scene.

ACT UP failed to march with Bailey's casket, but that did not stop Episalla from delivering her funeral speech. "Bill Clinton, we are here with Tim Bailey to remind you that while you continue to pay lip service to the AIDS crisis, the epidemic continues to rage on."

As the van slowly left the parking lot, a protester held a sign that said: "We Will Not Die in Peace. ACT UP."

"I am getting sicker. Time is running out."

New York Times reporter Jeffrey Schmalz was diagnosed as HIV-positive in early 1991, and for a while, he thought he might beat the disease. "Now, it is clear I will not," he wrote. The bleakness that his colleague Lawrence Altman had described was now descending on Schmalz.

"The treatments simply are not there," he explained. "They are not even in the pipeline." Sure, he could hope for a miracle. "But let's face it, a miracle isn't going to happen. One day soon I will become one of the 90 people in America to die that day of AIDS. It's like knowing I will be killed by a speeding car, but not knowing when or where."

Schmalz died on November 6, 1993, three weeks before his article was published. He was thirty-nine years old.

With drugs faltering, the Clinton administration ramped up an educational campaign as the best method for fighting the spread of HIV. In January 1994, the administration ran public service announcements, on television and radio, that advocated abstinence or the use of condoms to prevent the spread of HIV. It was an historic first. For more than ten years, the Reagan and Bush administrations had refused to run any ads mentioning condoms.

The ads were playful. One showed a wrapped condom popping out of a dresser drawer while a couple is close to having sex. The condom jumps to the floor, climbs the bed, and scoots under the blanket, apparently just in time.

The most popular AIDS educator in 1994 was not an animated condom but a handsome young man named Pedro Zamora, who starred in MTV's *The Real World*, a reality show that followed the lives of seven young people living in the same house.

Zamora, an HIV-positive AIDS educator, had no patience for tame responses to AIDS. Appearing before a congressional committee, he said, "I am frustrated with programs that are more concerned with offending people in the general public than with saving lives.

"If you want to reach me as a young gay man, especially a young gay man of color, then you need to give me the information in a language and vocabulary I can understand and relate to."

That's what Zamora did. He spoke to young people in direct and explicit language. He also used props—not wrapped condoms but open ones that he stretched across several fingers to show that no one was too big to use them. And because he had millions of fans—people of all classes and colors—no one reached more young people than Zamora did.

In June 1994, after he finished taping the last episode of *The Real World*, Zamora visited family and friends in Miami. He also crisscrossed

AIDS educator Pedro Zamora, far right.

the country, educating as many people as he could about the facts of HIV infection.

Four months later, he slipped into a coma and died. He was twenty-two years old.

What was left to do other than cry out in pain?

42

SHOCK AND AWE

MEMBERS OF THE TREATMENT ACTION GROUP (TAG) DECIDED TO LOOK FOR MORE drugs in the pipeline. But this time they used a new set of lenses.

In earlier years, TAG activists had pushed the FDA to ease its regulations and expedite the approval of AIDS drugs.

But the devastating news about AZT was a game changer. The drug had been rushed to the market, and rather than prolonging lives, it left many PWAs with little benefit and dreadful side effects.

So TAG members did a hard pivot. Now, they said, the FDA should not make AIDS drugs accessible unless it had strong evidence they worked over a long period of time.

The pivot was put to the test when Hoffman-La Roche, the manufacturer of a new AIDS drug, asked the FDA for accelerated approval. In August 1994, TAG members opposed granting permission until the company conducted a large trial that unquestionably proved the drug's safety and effectiveness.

The move shocked AIDS activists around the country, not just because TAG had pivoted away from its earlier stance, but also because the drug under consideration would be the first of its kind in the United

States—a protease inhibitor. It was the drug that Garance Franke-Ruta had mentioned during the 1990 storming of the NIH. If successful, the new drug would block protease—an enzyme essential to the life cycle of HIV—from acting and thereby stop HIV from spreading.

ACT UP member Bill Bahlman was furious about TAG's opposition to accelerated approval. "This is something we fought long and hard for," he told ACT UP. "We've been arrested to get accelerated approval through—many of us in this room were arrested to get that. We stormed the FDA!"

Treatment activists around the country also lined up against TAG. In San Francisco, Martin Delaney said, "People are not willing to go backward on the question of access."

None of the activists favored accelerated approval for drugs with flimsy data, but they did prefer a process that was far more streamlined than the one that TAG now supported.

TAG members dug in, and they convinced the FDA to hold off on approving the drug until Hoffman-La Roche offered more than substantial proof that it was safe and effective. The company subsequently conducted a six-month trial of 500 patients, and on December 7, 1995, the FDA approved the sale of the country's first protease inhibitor.

PWAs with financial resources rushed to their doctors and began taking this new source of hope. But before long, PWAs discovered that the drug's therapeutic benefits were short-lived and far from impressive. Another massive disappointment.

Bill Bahlman, co-founder of the Lavender Hill Mob and ACT UP.

Meanwhile, Merck & Co. was producing its own protease inhibitor—Crixivan.

Bill Bahlman was optimistic. As a member of Merck's community advisory board, he learned that Crixivan was proving effective at lowering "viral load," the amount of HIV in a person's bloodstream.

There was more good news, too. When Merck scientists combined

Crixivan with AZT, the results were even better than those produced by Crixivan alone. Using this combination therapy, the scientists saw a decrease in viral load and an increase in the number of CD4 cells—the cells that prevent infection.

Bahlman, an unfailing advocate for PWAs, urged Merck to seek early approval. "We can stop the dying!" he said. But Merck insisted that it needed a larger and lengthier trial to be sure of the drug's safety and effectiveness. With help from Bahlman and others, the new trial got underway in 1995.

Another trial for another protease inhibitor—named Retrovir—was also in process. This trial was designed by TAG member Spencer Cox and conducted by drugmaker Abbott Laboratories.

Cox, now vehemently opposed to accelerated approval, had designed a seven-month trial that randomly assigned thousands of people with HIV and AIDS to one of three groups: the first received a placebo, the second received a higher dose of the protease inhibitor, and the third received a lower dose.

For participants, one of the best aspects of the trial was that they did not have to stop taking their other drugs. But the trial was also controversial, at least among some activists, because it allowed for the use of a placebo, which meant that some participants would not receive any potential benefits of the protease inhibitor.

But Cox was adamant.

In January 1996, Emilio Emini, the director of Merck's research on Crixivan, walked on stage at the third annual Conference on Retroviruses and Opportunistic Infections.

He had seen his ups and downs when researching HIV and AIDS drugs. In one particularly low period, he had to tell Bill Bahlman that a drug he was in a clinical trial for had failed. It was a painful moment for both men; each held the other in high regard.

"What do you think I should do?" Emini asked, sounding disappointed and tired.

"Go home," Bahlman replied, "get a good night's sleep, and start tomorrow rededicated to your work."

Emini had labored on, and now the room was packed with scientists and activists eagerly awaiting his talk on the results of Merck's research. The moment was electric.

"We're seeing something that we've never seen before," Emini told the rapt audience. The scientist carefully explained that Crixivan, when combined with AZT and a similar drug, suppressed HIV to undetectable levels for at least six months.

Undetectable!

The audience was awestruck.

Even more good news arrived when Abbott Laboratories revealed in its own conference presentation that Retrovir, when used with AZT and a similar drug, cut AIDS deaths in half.

In half!

Merck's and Abbott's studies had limitations, and much more data was necessary for drawing definitive conclusions, but even the hypercautious Anthony Fauci declared that the early results were "impressive."

Spencer Cox was less restrained. "We did it," he said, tears streaming down his cheeks. "We're going to live."

Larry Kramer called his good friend, Dr. Larry Mass, with the news. The cofounders of the Gay Men's Health Crisis had long dreamed of this moment, and now that it was here, it was overwhelming.

Mass was speechless. The scientific achievement, he said later, was "mind-bogglingly miraculous, historical, and epochal."

Bill Bahlman had studied the safety and effectiveness of combination therapy, and he strongly urged the FDA to approve both Retrovir and Crixivan. In record time, the agency approved both drugs.

43

UNDETECTABLE

PETER STALEY AND HIS FRIENDS TOOK THE TRIPLE-DRUG COMBINATION AS SOON AS they could, and within thirty days, HIV became undetectable in their blood. "All of us," Staley said. "Undetectable, undetectable, undetectable."

They weren't alone. Undetectable cases were everywhere, and major publications began to report on PWAs who'd seen dramatic results.

Alicia had been in such poor health that she had thought about moving to a hospice. But now she was taking her dog for a two-mile walk.

Benjamin had been using an IV to feed himself because he could no longer ingest solid foods. But now he was planning to study for a master's degree.

Jill had been rejected from twelve drug trials because her AIDS was so advanced. But now she was devoting more time to AIDS activism—and even dating.

Carson had lost weight, went partially blind in his right eye, and developed KS lesions. "On paper I was a corpse," he said. But now he was running a marathon.

The virtually unbelievable results became known as the "Lazarus effect," a reference to the story in the Christian Bible about Jesus raising a dead man entombed in a cave:

> "Lazarus, come out!" The dead man came out, his hands and feet bound with strips of cloth and his face wrapped in a cloth. Jesus said to them, "Unbind him, and let him go."

For many, the miracle was real. HIV became undetectable, CD4 counts rose, and opportunistic infections disappeared. Mark Harrington saw Kaposi's sarcoma lesions "melting back" into his friend's skin.

FIGHT AIDS

Combination therapy—which is now known as antiretroviral therapy, or ART—was not without its problems. It was expensive. Its side effects could be very painful. It was ineffective if patients failed to follow the detailed directions for taking it. And it simply did not work in some patients, no matter what.

But when ART worked, HIV was no longer the killer virus.

FIGHT AIDS

"No obits."

The headline in the *Bay Area Reporter* was shocking. Since the start of the epidemic, the newspaper had published thousands of obituaries. In some issues, they ran for several pages. But today—August 13, 1998—there were none.

Not one.

"Wow," said Paul Wisotzky, who worked with the San Francisco AIDS Foundation. A few years earlier, he had stopped paying close attention to the obituaries because "my circle of friends died."

Reader Dana Van Gorder took the moment to reflect on all those who had suffered and fought to make this day happen. "We all deserve a little bit of respite," he said.

Front page of the *Bay Area Reporter*, August 13, 1998.

But Ronnie Burke, a member of ACT UP San Francisco, was critical of the headline and accompanying article. "The BAR [*Bay Area Reporter*] is not really a gauge of how many people died of AIDS in San Francisco. It is a gauge of how many white, middle-class men died."

The newspaper had already noted that in the week prior to the headline a homeless man with AIDS had died but no one had written an obituary for him. That acknowledgment, along with Burke's criticism, tempered the celebration.

The newspaper's editors, hardened by years of AIDS reporting, also acknowledged that future issues would no doubt include more obituaries. But they also dared to dream of a time when "no obits" would be common. "For that to happen," they said, "people must take care of themselves, avoid infections, and live for tomorrow."

With that, they ended on a hopeful note:

"See you around."

EPILOGUE

AN UNFINISHED LEGACY

ON NOVEMBER 7, 1991, EARVIN "MAGIC" JOHNSON JR., THE THIRTY-TWO-YEAR-OLD superstar of the Los Angeles Lakers, announced to a packed pressroom that he was HIV-positive. He was a beloved figure on and off the court, and tears filled the room as he shared the news. Even hardened journalists cried openly.

But Johnson was hopeful. "I plan on going on, living for a long time, bugging you guys, like I always have," he said.

Johnson's plan might have sounded like a pipe dream to those who knew the horrors of AIDS in 1991. After all, this was five years *before* the arrival of combination therapy.

But fast forward to today. Johnson is still alive—and still talking about living with HIV.

During the run-up to the 2024 Summer Olympics, he sat for an interview that revisited the shock of his HIV diagnosis. This time, Johnson spoke openly about the awful reality he'd faced in 1991. "HIV was a death sentence," he recalled, "and here I am, thirty-two years later."

Johnson has survived—and flourished. As a husband. A father. A business leader. And an AIDS activist. After his diagnosis, Johnson quickly joined the fight against AIDS, countering stigma, urging his fans to get tested for HIV, and lobbying the government for increased funding for housing and medicine and research. He focused much of his local work on Black and Brown communities.

Through the years, Johnson has cited various reasons for his survival—a strong support system, a positive outlook, access to the best

EPILOGUE

Volunteers advertising the Trilingual AIDS Hotline in San Francisco, 1994.

AIDS doctors and health care, and a fierce commitment to taking care of himself.

The survival, and flourishing, of Magic Johnson is also due to all the AIDS activists who fought so hard for safe and effective drugs. Johnson is a legacy of early AIDS activism in the United States.

And he's just one among *millions* of people whose lives have been—and will be—saved. These lives, visible in every corner of our country, also constitute the legacy of the men and women whose protests led to greater care, compassion, and acceptance for people with AIDS.

EPILOGUE

FIGHT AIDS

Their remarkable legacy is visible not only in millions of individual lives, but also in social groups, organizations, institutions, and our wider culture.

It's evident in medical research, where patient input is now actively sought, in the White House, which coordinates a national HIV/AIDS strategy, in Congress, which funds the Ryan White CARE Act, in the US Food and Drug Administration, which approves drugs faster and more efficiently, in public schools, which teach basic facts about HIV and AIDS, and in the wider culture, where the stigma of AIDS is no longer as pervasive as it once was.

AIDS activism has reshaped our nation—and even life far beyond our shores.

In 1996, the United Nations, inspired by activists in the United States and elsewhere, inaugurated UNAIDS, a campaign to eliminate AIDS as a global health threat. Seven years later, President George W. Bush established the President's Emergency Plan for AIDS Relief (PEPFAR), a health care initiative that targeted Africa. Thomas Sheehy of the United States Institute of Peace claims that in the years since its creation PEPFAR helped to "turn the tide on the global HIV pandemic" and saved 25 million lives.

AIDS activism has changed the world.

FIGHT AIDS

Challenges remain. They're not as massive as they might have been had AIDS activists not protested so forcefully in the 1980s and 1990s, but they're urgent, with millions of lives at stake.

Today, more than one million people in the United States have HIV.

About 30,000 people are infected each year, and the highest rates of infection are among Black Americans, Hispanic Americans, and people who live in poor communities.

The total number of new HIV infections and AIDS-related deaths throughout the world is decreasing. Still, about 40 million people are living with HIV, with more than a million becoming infected annually. The highest rates of infection are among girls and women in sub-Saharan Africa.

Discrimination against people with HIV also remains a painful reality. In most of the United States, it's legal for life and disability insurers to deny coverage to people with HIV.

FIGHT AIDS

Today's AIDS activists are trying to meet the challenge by working hard to ensure that all people, especially those in high-risk groups, have equal access to prevention methods and the best care available.

In New York City, the still-vibrant Gay Men's Health Crisis (GMHC) provides special programs and services for those disproportionately affected by HIV and AIDS—Black and Brown people, and transgender, gender-nonconforming, and nonbinary people. GMHC offers all clients a wide variety of services ranging from legal advice to help with errands. The San Francisco AIDS Foundation offers similar programs, including one that allows eligible people to receive prescriptions for the preventive drug called PrEP.

Direct-action protests continue, too.

In July 2024, an international coalition of activists staged a protest at the 25th International AIDS Conference in Munich, Germany. The protesters were pleased with recent reports about a new way to prevent HIV infections—by getting a twice-yearly injection of a drug called lenacapavir. But like ACT UP years earlier, they were concerned about the cost and availability of the drug. Carrying handmade signs, the coalition demanded that Gilead Sciences, the manufacturer of lenacapavir, make the drug affordable and accessible, especially to people in poorer countries.

FIGHT AIDS

But the legacy of the first AIDS activists remains unfinished.

One new HIV infection occurs every 24 seconds.

There is insufficient health care.

There is no vaccine.

There is no cure.

And so the battle cry continues—

Fight AIDS!

ACKNOWLEDGMENTS

My deepest thanks to all the ordinary people who sacrificed so much, sometimes their very lives, in the historic fight against HIV and AIDS. Their extraordinary acts of courage and compassion inspire me daily, and I could not be more honored than I am to share their stories.

Many thanks to my superb editor at Norton Young Readers, Simon Boughton. This book was his idea, and I am still thrilled that he asked me to write it. Simon is a creative visionary with a big heart, and working with him has been delightful.

My experience with Norton has been wonderful, and my gratitude extends to the excellent team behind this book: Hana Anouk Nakamura (Art Director and designer), Kristin Allard (Assistant Editor), Naomi Duttweiler (Marketing Manager), Rebecca Springer (Managing Editor), Delaney Adams (Production Manager), and Renata Mitchell (Senior Counsel).

I am happily indebted to John Rudolph, of Dystel, Goderich & Bourret, for connecting me with Simon and Norton, and for sharing his counsel through the years. John is not only an agent of agents—he's also a good friend.

Hey! A special shout-out to Dr. Larry Mass, Bill Bahlman, Helen Scheitinger, Perry Brass, Philip Gefter, Andy Humm, Hal Moskowitz, and Jim Geary for giving me such rich insight into the people, places and events in the AIDS fight. Such eye-opening conversations!

May I tell you how much I appreciate librarians and archivists? For their help with this book, I am grateful for the staff at the Manuscript and Archives Division of the New York Public Library, the GLBT Historical Society Museum and Archives, and the Library of Congress.

The artwork of this book is breathtaking, and I refer you to the credits for a list of all the good people who helped me with images. ACT UP New York was especially kind and generous in granting me permission to publish pieces from their collection.

I have drawn the stories of this book from numerous sources—conversations, interviews, articles, films, books, and more. Although the notes cite only those sources that I have directly quoted, many others played a vital role. Two outstanding books served an outsized role in helping me set scenes: Randy Shilts's *And the Band Played On: Politics, People, and the AIDS Epidemic*, and David France's *How to Survive a Plague: The Story of How Activists and Scientists Tamed AIDS*. Special thanks to Shilts (now deceased) and France.

My family and friends are super cool and supportive. So big hugs to a bunch of Longs—Karin, Jack, Elda, Nate, Bob, and George—and to friends Sharon Herr, who proofread several versions of the manuscript, and Shea Tuttle.

Finally, I thank all my young readers for your interest in this largely untaught subject. May you draw inspiration from the everyday heroes of this book and join them in the cry that remains as important now as ever—

Fight AIDS!

NOTES

Basic Facts
7 **"What is HIV?"**: Centers for Disease Control and Prevention, *About HIV*, January 24, 2024, https://www.cdc.gov/hiv/about/index.html. Some of the chapter's bulleted information has been condensed and revised for clarity.

1. Stonewall
7 **"Police"**: David Carter, *Stonewall: The Riots That Sparked the Gay Revolution* (St. Martin's Griffin, 2004), 137. Segal's part of the story is in Mark Segal, *And Then I Danced: Traveling the Road to LGBT Equality* (Akashik, 2015), 29–53.
8 **"unnatural attire"**: Rick Bragg, "From a Night of Rage, the Seeds of Liberation," *New York Times*, June 23, 1994.
8 **"the queens"**: Carter, *Stonewall*, 148.
9 **"Why don't you"**: Carter, *Stonewall*, 151.
9 **"Pigs!"**: *Stonewall Uprising*, directed by Kate Davis and David Heilbroner, produced by Mark Samels, Kate Davis, David Heilbroner, and Sharon Grimberg, 2010, aired June 10, 2023, on PBS, https://www.pbs.org/wgbh/americanexperience/films/stonewall.
9 **"I wanted to kill"**: *Stonewall Uprising*, Davis and Heilbroner, 2010.
10 **"We all had a collective"**: Carter, *Stonewall*, 160.
10 **"Gay power!"**: Martin Duberman, *Stonewall: The Definitive Story of the LGBTQ Rights Uprising That Changed America* (Plume, 2019), 250; and Carter, *Stonewall*, 184.
11 **"The nights of Friday"**: Craig Rodwell, "Get the Mafia and the Cops Out of Gay Bars," quoted in Elizabeth A. Armstrong and Suzanna M. Crage, "Movements and Memory: The Making of the Stonewall Myth," *American Sociological Review* 71.5 (October 2006): 738.

2. Sexual Liberation
12 **"a toilet"**: Perry Brass, in discussion with the author, October 2, 2023.
12 **"sexual liberation"**: Quoted in Lillian Faderman, *The Gay Revolution: The Story of the Struggle* (Simon & Schuster, 2015), 199.
13 **"orgy room" and "like having a"**: Brass, discussion, October 2, 2023.
14 **"Yes, I guess" and "Hell, you should"**: Perry Brass, "Sterility and Homosex-

uality," *Come Out: A Liberation Forum for the Gay Community* 2.7b (Spring–Summer 1971): 11.

3. Do-It-Yourself Health Care

15 **"Oh, my god!":** Perry Brass, in discussion with the author, October 2, 2023.
18 **"A few men" and "We got men":** Perry Brass, "A Prophecy Before Our Time: The Gay Men's Health Project Clinic Opens in 1972, Part Two: A Wasted Opportunity," New York Public Library, December 20, 2013, https://live-legacy-admin.nypl.org/blog/2013/12/20/mens-health-project-clinic-opens-wasted-opportunity.
19 **"This is really":** Brass, discussion, October 2, 2023.

4. A Chef, a Nurse, and a Teacher

25 **"Donna, you're not":** Ronald Bayer and Gerald M. Oppenheimer, *AIDS Doctors: Voices from the Epidemic—An Oral History* (Oxford University Press, 2000), 13.

5. Sharing the News

27 **"My doctor is Larry Downs":** Larry Mass, "The Housemate Who Got Nailed," no date, Lawrence Mass Papers, 1958–2008, New York Public Library, New York City, box 4.
27 **"They told me" and "Well, there were":** Lawrence Mass, in discussion with the author, July 19, 2023.
28 **"Last week," "Each year," "obviously compromised," and "But of the eleven":** Lawrence Mass, "Disease Rumors Largely Unfounded," *New York Native*, May 18, 1981. Remaining chapter quotations are drawn from this source.

6. More Pneumonia, More Cancer

31 **"Rare Cancer Seen," "appears in one," and "According to Dr.":** Lawrence K. Altman, "Rare Cancer Seen in 41 Homosexuals," *New York Times*, July 3, 1981. All article quotations come from this source.
32 **"What did these guys":** Eric Marcus, "Coming of Age During the AIDS Crisis—Chapter 1," *Making Gay History: The Podcast*, no date, https://makinggayhistory.org/podcast/coming-of-age-during-the-aids-crisis-chapter-1.
33 **"seemed like a new" and "seemed like just":** David France, *How to Survive a Plague: The Story of How Activists and Scientists Tamed AIDS* (Vintage, 2016), 14.
33 **"What the fuck?" and "We're lepers again":** Philip Gefter, in discussion with the author, September 21, 2023.

NOTES

34 **"We're only seeing" and "I don't think":** France, *How to Survive a Plague*, 22.

7. Raising Money

35 **"can't be overridingly," "cuts and abrasions," and "At this time":** Lawrence Mass, "Cancer Strikes the Gay Community," *New York Native*, July 24, 1981.
36 **"You could have":** Andy Humm, in discussion with the author, August 25, 2023.
36 **"communicable" and "gay sexual activity":** Humm reading notes taken from meeting, Andy Humm, in discussion with the author, September 21, 2023.
37 **"It's difficult to write" and "This is our":** Larry Kramer, "A Personal Appeal," *New York Native*, August 24, 1981.

8. Bobbi Hangs a Poster

42 **"I was stricken":** "I Will Survive," June 19, 1983, radio interview, KPFK, Los Angeles, California, June 19, 1983.
42 **"I'm Bobbi Campbell," "Since I'm a professional," "What I found," "a support group," and "Kaposi's Sarcoma":** Bobbi Campbell, "I Will Survive," *San Francisco Sentinel*, December 10, 1981.
44 **"GAY CANCER" and "big purple splotches":** Poster visible in *We Were Here*, directed by David Weissman, produced by David Weissman Productions, 2011.

9. Emotional Support

47 **"While we have," "Topics for conversation," "It's been known," and "We form":** Bobbi Campbell, "Gay Cancer Journal: KS Support Group," *San Francisco Sentinel*, April 15, 1982.

10. Traci Gets a Buddy

50 **"Gay men certainly do," "Let's use that," and "because it showed":** Jeff Graham, "1981–1986: In the Beginning," TheBody.com, February 1, 2006.
51 **"I had a hundred," "I mean," "We had a":** "McFarlane, Rodger," Gay Men's Health Crisis Records, New York Public Library, Manuscripts and Archives Division, New York City, Part XVI.C, Oral Histories, 204028; and Paul Schindler, "Rodger McFarlane, AIDS, Gay Community Builder, Dead at 54," *Gay City News*, May 30, 2009.
52 **"Of course," "Oh, my God," "She was Latinx," "I'm not a drag," "I'm not a drug," "The cause of death":** Hal Moskowitz, in discussion with the author, October 26, 2023.

11. From GRID to AIDS

56 **"the epidemic was" and "strongly suggested":** James W. Curran and Harold W. Jaffe, "AIDS: The Early Years and CDC's Response," *Morbidity and Mortality Weekly Report* 60.4 (October 7, 2011): 64–69. For more on the "one gay man," Gaetan Dugas, erroneously referred to as "Patient Zero" in Randy Shilts, *And the Band Played On: Politics, People, and the Epidemic* (St. Martin's Press, 1987), 23, see Richard A. McKay, *Patient Zero and the Making of the AIDS Epidemic* (University of Chicago Press, 2017).

57 **"GRID" and "homosexual disorder":** Lawrence K. Altman, "New Homosexual Disorder Worries Health Officials," *New York Times*, May 11, 1982.

57 **"gay plague":** Curran and Jaffe, "AIDS," October 7, 2011.

58 **"AIDS," "risk factors" and "AIDS cases":** "Current Trends Update on Acquired Immune Deficiency Syndrome (AIDS)—United States," *Morbidity and Mortality Weekly Report* 31.37 (September 24, 1982): 507–8, 513–14.

58 **"unexplained cellular":** "Possible Transfusion-Associated Acquired Immune Deficiency Syndrome (AIDS)—California," *Morbidity and Mortality Weekly Report* 31.48 (December 10, 1982): 652–54.

12. Calling for Condoms

59 **"promiscuity" and "We Know":** Richard Berkowitz and Michael Callen, "We Know Who We Are: Two Men Declare War on Promiscuity," *New York Native*, November 8, 1982.

60 **"Tom wanted sex," "It was a moment," "How to Have":** Richard Berkowitz, *Stayin' Alive: The Invention of Safe Sex—A Personal History* (Westview Press, 2003), 139–41.

61 **"to interrupt disease":** *Sex Positive*, directed by Daryl Wein, produced by David Oliver Cohen, Daryl Wein, and Zoe Lister Jones, 2008.

62 **"I read through it":** David France, *How to Survive a Plague: The Story of How Activists and Scientists Tamed AIDS* (Vintage Books, 2016), 98. France was reading Richard Berkowitz and Michael Callen, *How to Have Sex in an Epidemic: One Approach* (News from the Front Publications, 1983).

62 **"They were everywhere":** France, *How to Survive a Plague*, 99.

13. The Missing White House

64 **"In the gay community," "I don't know," "Oh, we've done," "We are training," and "We don't feel":** "Larry Kramer 1982 Interview on AIDS," September 28, 1982, 13:48, posted by SuchIsLifeVideos, 2014, https://www.youtube.com/watch?v=Lda9YhshTV4.

65 "Larry, does the," "What's," "Over a third," "No, it is," "I don't have it," "You don't," "Do you," "No," "How do you," "Well, I just," "No, I don't," "Does the president," "I don't think," "Nobody knows," "There has been": *Vanity Fair*, "Reagan Administration's Chilling Response to the AIDS Crisis," video, 7:43, posted December 1, 2015, https://www.youtube.com/watch?v=yAzDn7tE1lU.

14. Taking It to the Streets

71 "Unless we fight," "There are now," "We are learning how," "I hope we don't": Larry Kramer, "1,112 and Counting," *New York Native*, March 14, 1983.

72 "Somebody should do": *A Time of Change: Confronting AIDS*, directed and produced by Mark Decker and Al LaValley, 1986.

72 "honor the dead": "An AIDS Candlelight March," flyer, May 2, 1983, University of California, San Francisco Archives & Special Collections, 1973, 1981–2002, box 7, folder 9.

73 "The church, family": Dave Marez, "Castro District, San Francisco," *The AIDS Memorial*, Facebook, posted May 2, 2022.

73 "Fighting for Our Lives" and "Our president doesn't": Randy Shilts, "S.F. Procession to Dramatize AIDS," *San Francisco Chronicle*, May 3, 1983.

73 "patient" and "victim": "March for AIDS Draws Large Crowd," *Bay Area Reporter*, May 5, 1983.

73 "I am defining myself": Miles W. Griffis, "How the 'Magna Carta of AIDS Activism' Sparked a Revolution," NationalGeographic.com, June 7, 2023.

74 "If one of us": Decker and LaValley, *A Time of Change*, 1986.

15. People with AIDS

75 "BE IT RESOLVED": Bobbi Campbell, "S.F. AIDS Alliance," *San Francisco Sentinel*, May 26, 1983.

76 "It just fueled us" and "Fighting for Our Lives": Mathew Rodriguez, "Remembering the Denver Principles, 40 Years Later," TheBody.com, July 5, 2023.

77 "We condemn attempts," "our struggle against," "be involved at," "full and satisfying," "die—and live": *The Denver Principles*, UNAIDS.com, June 1983.

16. A Revolution on Ward 5B

79 "I wonder how," "Before I got," "It's scary": "AIDS," *20/20*, ABC News, May 19, 1983. Posted at "AIDS, 20/20, 5/19/83," Vimeo.com, 2018, video, 16:51, https://vimeo.com/269698918.

79 **"The plaza was" and "horror flick":** David France, *How to Survive a Plague: The Story of How Activists and Scientists Tamed AIDS* (Vintage, 2016), 91.

80 **"spacesuits":** *5B*, directed by Dan Kraus and Paul Haggis, produced by Dan Kraus, Brendan Gaul, Rupert Maconick, Paul Haggis, Guru Gowrappan, Hayley Pappas, and Brett Henenberg, Saville Productions, 2018.

80 **"leper colony":** Katherine Bishop, "Ward 5B: A Model of Care for AIDS," *New York Times*, December 14, 1985.

81 **"Tell me what" and "I want to":** Cliff Morrison, as told to Brooke Porter Katz, "'They Needed to Feel Loved': How One Nurse Revolutionized Patient Care During the AIDS Crisis," JNJ.com, June 7, 2019.

81 **"You're probably going," "Yeah, I might," "We were young," "And they were," "You have to get," "People need," "I had no," "Here you were":** *5B*, directed by Kraus and Haggis, 2018.

83 **"the San Francisco model":** Morrison and Katz, "'They Need to Feel Loved,'" June 7, 2019.

17. Dying and Discovering

84 **"I can feel it," "Love really":** Decker and LaValley, *A Time of Change*, 1986; and "Psychologist Succumbs to AIDS," *Bay Area Reporter*, March 18, 1984.

84 **"When you violate," "My God," "Gary has nothing," "I'm quite a," "curing":** Randy Shilts, *And the Band Played On*, 347–48.

85 **"His legacy":** "Psychologist Succumbs to AIDS," March 18, 1984.

85 **"The probable cause," "a blood test," and "We'll also be":** A transcript of Heckler's comments is available online at "Margaret Heckler: Press Conference," April 23, 1984, Jon Cohen AIDS Research Collection, University of Michigan Library Digital Collections, quod.lib.mich.edu.

86 **"If a man thinks":** "HIV Turns 30 Today," AbcNews.Go.com, April 23, 2013.

87 **"Holy mackerel!":** Ivan Sharpe, *San Francisco Examiner*, July 16, 1984.

88 **"medical nightmare":** John M. Leighty, "Gay Power at Demo Convention," UPI news story, March 10, 1984, UPI.com.

88 **"the two thousand," "We need increased," "Homosexuality does not," and "Keep the faith":** Bobbi Campbell, untitled speech, July 15, 1984. A video of this speech is available at "Bobbi Campbell Speech," 2:14, https://www.youtube.com/watch?v=mR2uMoGO6Xk.

18. The Bathhouse Battles

90 **"Hurry up, doc":** Leon Neyfakh, Andrew Parsons, Sam Graham-Felsen, Madeline Kaplan, Ula Kulpa, Prologue Projects, *The Baths*, episode 3, *Fiasco: The AIDS Crisis*, Audible Original Podcast, 2023.

NOTES

90 **"the most dirty"**: "Jerry Falwell and Troy Perry Debate the Morality of AIDS," *The Journal*, CBC, 1983, video, 8:27, https://www.cbc.ca/player/play/video/1.3332889.

91 **"I don't want legislation"**: Allen White, "Milkers Toss Pot Around Bathhouse Closure," *Bay Area Reporter*, March 29, 1984.

91 **"We will be taking steps"**: Evelyn Hsu, "S.F. Orders Ban on Sex in Bathhouses," *San Francisco Chronicle*, April 10, 1984.

92 **"glory holes"**: George Mendenhall, "Sex Banned in Sex Palaces with Gay Backing," *Bay Area Reporter*, April 12, 1984.

92 **"literally playing Russian"**: Carl Nolte and Randy Shilts, "Gay Bathhouses Told to Close—6 Refuse," *San Francisco Chronicle*, October 10, 1984.

92 **"baths closure is"** and **"Keep the City"**: George Mendenhall, "300 at Rally to Decry Baths Closure," *Bay Area Reporter*, November 1, 1984.

19. A Hollywood Heartthrob

97 **"You're too thin"**: James Kirchick, *Secret City: The Hidden History of Gay Washington* (Henry Holt, 2022), 569.

98 **"It's Kaposi's sarcoma"**: Kirchick, *Secret City*, 570.

99 **"This has been," "That's what they,"** and **"Mr. Rock Hudson"**: *Rock Hudson: All That Heaven Allowed*, directed by Stephen Kijak, 2023.

101 **"Scientific advances"**: Robert Pear, "U.S. Seeks Increase in AIDS Research Funds," *New York Times*, July 29, 1985.

20. A Midwestern Teen

102 **"Am I gonna," "We're all gonna"**: Jeanne White Ginder, interviewed by Allen Safianow, Ryan White Oral History Project, Howard County Historical Society, Kokomo, Indiana, October 28, 2014; quoted in Taylor Dickinson, "'When I Die, Please Don't Bury Me in Kokomo,'" senior thesis, Butler University, no date.

103 **"With all the things"** and **"I'm pretty upset"**: Mark Nichols, "Young AIDS Victim Barred from School," *Indianapolis Star*, July 31, 1985.

104 **"The hemophiliacs"** and **"I'm not mad"**: John Norberg, *Journal and Carrier* (Lafayette, Indiana), March 14, 1985. For more on Ryan as "innocent," see Paul Renfro, "Ryan White, Teen Who Contracted AIDS, Shifted Narrative Around the Disease," *Teen Vogue*, December 6, 2021.

105 **"Based on current"**: "Current Trends: Education and Foster Care of Children Infected with Human T-Lymphotropic Virus Type III/Lymphadenopathy-Associated Virus," *Morbidity and Mortality Report*, August 30, 1985.

105 **"a massive government," "a top priority," "If you had,"** and **"I'm glad I'm"**:

"The President's News Conference," September 17, 1985, Ronald Reagan Presidential Library & Museum, ReaganLibrary.gov.

21. Positive Change, Creative Protest

107 **"He is a"**: Michael Collins, "Actor Hudson, Apparently Unresponsive to Treatment in Paris," UPI news story, July 30, 1985, UPI.com.

107 **"love and support"**: Randy Shilts, "Hollywood's Glittering AIDS Benefit—Star-Studded Show Raises $1 Million," *San Francisco Chronicle*, September 20, 1985.

108 **"remarkable progress" and "I am not"**: "Doris Day Helped America Look at AIDS with Empathy and Love for Rock Hudson," *New York Times*, May 13, 2019.

108 **"a sharply increased"**: Randy Shilts, "Hudson's Contribution to AIDS Battle," *San Francisco Chronicle*, October 3, 1985.

109 **"Are you handing" and "Why don't you?"**: Allen White, "Protesters Attacked at Federal Bldg. AIDS Vigil," *Bay Area Reporter*, November 7, 1985.

22. Corpses Everywhere

111 **"I wish we"**: Cleve Jones with Jeff Dawson, *Stitching a Revolution: The Making of an Activist* (HarperSanFrancisco, 2000), 105.

112 **"There's a more"**: "Gay Vigil Marks Deaths of the Past and Present," *San Francisco Chronicle*, November 28, 1985.

112 **"I stood" and "We send"**: "Text of Speech by Cleve Jones," *San Francisco Sentinel*, December 5, 1985.

113 **"Stop AIDS now!"**: Jones with Dawson, *Stitching a Revolution*, 106.

113 **"Standing in the drizzle" and "And as I"**: Jones with Dawson, *Stitching a Revolution*, 107.

114 **"But I was on"**: Jones with Dawson, *Stitching a Revolution*, 109.

23. Blood Tests, Blood Sisters

116 **"We felt that," "based on blatant," and "It [Spindler's act]"**: Kristina Lindgren, "Fear of AIDS Leads Red Cross to Cancel Lesbian Drive," *Los Angeles Times*, January 9, 1985.

24. AZT Arrives

121 This chapter's account of the AZT trials is indebted to David France, *How to Survive a Plague: The Story of How Activists and Scientists Tamed AIDS* (Vintage, 2016), 180 and following.

25. Buyers' Clubs

124 **"He looked like"**: John Rhodes, "Miracle of Miracles?" *New York Daily News*, March 29, 1987.

126 **"government indifference and bureaucratic sluggishness"**: David Holmberg, "Relief for AIDS Claimed," *New York Daily News*, May 5, 1987. For the account of Stephen Roach and Praxis Pharmaceuticals, see David France, *How to Survive a Plague: The Story of How Activists and Scientists Tamed AIDS* (Vintage, 2016), 256–57.

127 **"It's useless"**: France, *How to Survive a Plague*, 262.

127 **"Please, I *beg*"**: France, *How to Survive a Plague*, 264–65.

26. The Mob Screams

128 **"Everyone detected with"**: William F. Buckley, Jr., "Crucial Steps in Combating the AIDS Epidemic," *New York Times*, March 18, 1986.

129 **"AIDS"**: Bruce Michael Gelbert, "Remember When Buckley Wanted to Tattoo PWAs?" *New York Q News*, no date.

129 **"We're going, and"**: Dudley Clendinen and Adam Nagourney, *Out for Good: The Struggle to Build a Gay Rights Movement in America* (Simon & Schuster, 1999), 543.

130 **"Centers for Detention" and "inept and murderous"**: Michele Cohen, "Experts Grapple with Ethics of AIDS Testing," *South Florida Sentinel*, February 25, 1987.

131 **"I'm wearing this"**: Steve Sternberg, "Mandatory AIDS Testing Draws 'Little Support,'" *Atlanta Constitution*, February 25, 1987.

131 **"You've sold out," "We should be," and "I think you"**: Clendinen and Nagourney, *Out for Good*, 543–44.

132 **"You're just like"**: Edward Edelson, "Gay 'Mob' Strikes Parley," *New York Daily News*, February 26, 1987.

132 **"We're tired"**: Clendinen and Nagourney, *Out for Good*, 543; and David Holmberg, "Support for Law Banning AIDS Bias," *New York Newsday*, February 26, 1987.

27. SILENCE = DEATH

134 **"I can either"**: Theodore Kerr, "How Six NYC Activists Changed History with 'SILENCE = DEATH,'" *Village Voice*, June 20, 2017.

135 **"when New Yorkers"**: Avram Finkelstein, "The SILENCE = DEATH Poster," blog post, *LGBTQ at NYPL*, November 22, 2013.

135 **"poster needed"**: Avram Finkelstein, *After Silence: A History of AIDS Through Its Images* (University of California Press, 2018), 40.

135 **"Women were coming down"**: Kerr, "How Six NYC Activists Changed History with 'SILENCE = DEATH,'" June 20, 2017.
135 **"inherently exclusionary"**: Finkelstein, *After Silence*, 43.
136 **"potentially disempowering" and "But we gave"**: Finkelstein, *After Silence*, 44–45.
136 **"Why is Reagan"**: See poster copy at "'SILENCE = DEATH' Poster," NYPL.org.
136 **"SILENCE = Death"**: Finkelstein, *After Silence*, 45.

28. ACT UP!

139 **"I'd like to"**: Michael Petrelis, interviewed by Sarah Schulman, April 21, 2003, ACT UP Oral History Project: A Program of MIX—The New York Lesbian & Gay Experimental Film Festival, Inc., actuporalhistory.org.
139 **"blood"**: Frank Rich, "'The Normal Heart,' By Larry Kramer," *New York Times*, April 22, 1985.
139 **"Don't worry"**: Petrelis, Schulman interview, April 21, 2003.
140 **"Just fucking be"**: Andy Humm, in discussion with the author, August 25, 2023.
141 **"I would like," "At the rate," "If my speech," "Give us," "They protested," "central organization"**: Larry Kramer, *Reports from the Holocaust: The Story of an AIDS Activist*, updated and expanded edition (St. Martin's Press, 1984), 127–36.
142 **"no more business"**: Ron Goldberg, *Boy with the Bullhorn: A Memoir and History of ACT UP New York* (Empire State Editions, 2000), 14.
142 **"CAN, Cure AIDS"**: Dudley Clendinen and Adam Nagourney, *Out for Good: The Struggle to Build a Gay Rights Movement in America* (Simon & Schuster, 1999), 555.
142 **"AIDS Coalition"**: Goldberg, *Boy with the Bullhorn*, 14.
142 **"ACT UP"**: Sarah Schulman, *Let the Record Show: A Political History of ACT UP New York, 1987–1993* (Farrar, Straus and Giroux, 2021), 325.
142 **"AIDS Coalition to Unleash Power"**: Goldberg, *Boy with the Bullhorn*, 14–15. Goldberg's account suggests that Bohrer pitched the acronym and the full name. It also includes the information about the name sounding like a toothpaste.
143 **"Immediate release"**: "NO MORE BUSINESS AS USUAL," flyer, no date [March 1987], actupny.org.
143 **"We are angry"**: "Detailed Scene List and Transcription," no date, actupny.org.
143 **"We're basically protesting" and "Such greed"**: Frances McMorris, "Gays Urge AIDS Drugs," *New York Daily News*, March 25, 1987.

NOTES

144 **"Getting arrested"**: "Cops Arrest 17 in AIDS Drugs Protest," *New York Newsday*, March 25, 1987.

29. The AIDS Quilt

149 **"Too many goddamn" and "Faggot"**: Jones with Dawson, *Stitching a Revolution*, 115–16.

149 **"It was just" and "Gay people"**: Judy Tachibana, "Activist's Knifing Called Part of Anti-Gay Trend," *Sacramento Bee*, May 31, 1986.

149 **"I was consumed"**: Jones with Dawson, *Stitching a Revolution*, 117.

150 **"I felt like"**: Jones with Dawson, *Stitching a Revolution*, 120.

151 **"Something about working" and "People just started"**: "Memorial Quilt Rolls Out," *New York Times*, October 12, 1987.

152 **"No, they're taking"**: Candy J. Cooper, "Tons of Cloth, Thousands of Memories in Quilt," *San Francisco Examiner*, October 12, 1987.

152 **"Marvin Feldman"**: Jones with Dawson, *Stitching a Revolution*, 123.

152 **"outrage that there," "It's pretty painful," "Life's not supposed"**: Cooper, "Tons of Cloth, Thousands of Memories in Quilt."

154 **"I have decorated"**: "The AIDS Memorial," *New York Times*, October 14, 1987.

154 **"locks of hair"**: Jones with Dawson, *Stitching a Revolution*, 134.

154 **"Nancy"**: Katherine Bishop, "Denying AIDS Its Sting," *New York Times*, October 5, 1987.

154 **"You Are My"**: John Johnson, "Quilt's Stitches Tie Memories of Lives Lost to AIDS," *Sacramento Bee*, October 12, 1987.

154 **"This is simultaneously"**: Cooper, "Tons of Cloth, Thousands of Memories in Quilt," October 12, 1987.

154 **"It's one response"**: Jones with Dawson, *Stitching a Revolution*, 127.

30. The Largest Protest

155 **"I have AIDS"**: Carl M. Cannon and Bart Greenwald, "Thousands March for Gay Rights," *Philadelphia Inquirer*, October 12, 1987.

155 **"For some of these"**: Mike Connolly, "Festive Mood at Gay Parade in Washington," *San Francisco Examiner*, October 12, 1987.

155 **"Shame, shame, shame!"**: Randy Shilts, "Hundreds of Thousands March," *San Francisco Chronicle*, October 12, 1987.

156 **"Act up!"**: Marc Stein, "Memories of the 1987 March on Washington," outhistory.org, August 2013.

156 **"AIDSGATE" and "This Political Scandal"**: See copy in Jack Lowery, *It Was Vulgar & It Was Beautiful: How AIDS Activists Used Art to Fight a Pandemic* (Bold Type Books, 2022), 59.

NOTES

157 **"How many more"**: Doris Sue Wong, "200,000 Gays and Supporters Rally in Washington to Press for Rights," *Boston Globe*, October 12, 1987.

157 **"Mr. President, did"**: Shilts, "Hundreds of Thousands March," October 12, 1987.

157 **"We have AIDS"**: Lena Williams, "600 in Gay Demonstration Arrested at Supreme Court," *New York Times*, October 14, 1987.

158 **"A lot of us"**: Karlyn Barker and Linda Wheeler, "Gay Activists Arrested at High Court," *Washington Post*, October 14, 1987.

158 **"The events all fit"**: "600 Protesters for Gay Rights Arrested Outside the Court," *San Francisco Chronicle*, October 14, 1987.

31. Ryan White Testifies

159 **"Because of a lack" and "the lies about me"**: Tim Franklin, "At 13, 'Face to Face with Death,'" *Philadelphia Daily News*, March 4, 1988.

161 **"When he [Ryan]"**: Dirk Johnson, "Ryan White Dies of AIDS," *New York Times*, April 9, 1990.

161 **"For the first time" and "I'm just one"**: Franklin, "At 13, 'Face to Face with Death,'" March 4, 1988; and Lindsey Beckley, "Overcoming Stigma: Ryan White, Hamilton Heights, and Tony Cook's Educational Crusade," *Untold Indiana*, blog.history.in.gov, August 29, 2019.

162 **"The White House"**: Margaret Carlson, "A Doctor Prescribes Hard Truth: C. Everett Koop," *TIME*, April 24, 1989.

162 **"condoms have been"**: "U.S. Will Mail AIDS Advisory to All Households," *New York Times*, May 5, 1988.

162 **"embarrassed"**: Philip M. Boffey, "F.D.A. Budget for AIDS Called Too Low," *New York Times*, February 20, 1988.

163 **"distinct lack of" and "the most significant obstacle"**: Sara G. Boodman, "Commission's Chief Faults AIDS Response," *Washington Post*, June 3, 1988.

163 **"People will simply"**: "AIDS Panel Urges Antibias Laws," *Chicago Tribune*, June 3, 1988.

164 **"I believe the"**: Sally Squires, "Setting the Course on AIDS," *Washington Post*, June 7, 1988.

164 **"The report embraces"**: Julie Johnson, "Report by AIDS Panel Gets Muted Reaction by Reagan," *New York Times*, June 28, 1988.

32. Seize Control of the FDA!

169 **"We need to seize"**: David France, *How to Survive a Plague: The Story of How Activists and Scientists Tamed AIDS* (Vintage, 2016), 324.

170 **"Act up!"**: Ron Goldberg, *Boy with the Bullhorn: A Memoir and History of ACT UP New York* (Empire State Editions, 2000), 128.
170 **"AZT is not," "Drugs for sale," "Seize control," "We're not asking," "I'm here," "Time Isn't," "We recognize," "Guilty!"**: "Seize Control of the FDA," video, ACT UP Oral History Project, actuporalhistory.org.
172 **"1,000 Swarm"**: "1,000 Swarm FDA's Rockville Office to Demand Approval of AIDS Drugs," *Washington Post*, October 12, 1988.

33. Dropping Prices, Exchanging Needles

174 **"the parallel track"**: Gina Kolata, "AIDS Researcher Seeks Wide Access to Drugs in Tests," *New York Times*, June 26, 1989.
176 **"Sell Wellcome"**: "AIDS Activists Arrested at Stock Exchange," UPI news story, September 14, 1989, UPI.com.
176 **"We die"**: David France, *How to Survive a Plague: The Story of How Activists and Scientists Tamed AIDS* (Vintage, 2016), 381.
176 **"DIE, FAGGOTS!"**: David Handelman, "Act Up in Anger," *Rolling Stone*, March 8, 1990.
177 **"The best way"**: "$20M More for AIDS Drugs," *New York Newsday*, September 14, 1989.
177 **"a pretty strong indication"**: Philip J. Hilts, "AIDS Drug's Maker Cuts Price by 20%," *New York Times*, September 19, 1989.
177 **"Sometimes I feel" and "Jon's saved"**: Catherine Woodard, "Against AIDS, 'the Works,'" *New York Newsday*, March 5, 1990.
178 **"We're trying to save"**: Bruce Lambert, "10 Seized in Demonstration as They Offer New Needles," *New York Times*, March 7, 1990.

34. Storm the NIH!

180 **"Open all decision"**: David France, *How to Survive a Plague: The Story of How Activists and Scientists Tamed AIDS* (Vintage, 2016), 409–10. The first part of this chapter is drawn from 400–410.
181 **"We're Fired," "Act up," "AZT Is Not," "invisible," "This is a story," "I have a home"**: "Storm the NIH," video, ACT UP Oral History Project, actuporalhistory.org.
183 **"It was interesting"**: Veronica T. Jennings and Malcolm Gladwell, "1,000 Rally for More Vigorous AIDS Effort," *Washington Post*, May 22, 1990.
183 **"protease inhibitors"**: "Storm the NIH," ACT UP Oral History Project, actuporalhistory.org.

35. Wins and Losses

185 **"Guilty!"**: Gretchen Kell and Deborah Blum, "Scientists, Activists Bash US Policy on AIDS," *Sacramento Bee*, June 21, 1990.

185 **"If you believe," "Change the law," "Can we all"**: "Peter Staley Speech at the Sixth International Conference on AIDS," June 20, 1990, video, 14:23, SuchIsLifeVideos, 2005. https://www.youtube.com/watch?v=Vn8qEjPnoSo.

186 **"obstruct the flow"**: Janny Scott, "Arrests, Pleas Mark Opening of AIDS Talks," *Los Angeles Times*, June 21, 1990.

186 **"After 10 years" and "He Talks, We Die"**: Ron Goldberg, *Boy with the Bullhorn: A Memoir and History of ACT UP New York* (Empire State Editions, 2000), 276.

187 **"We die"**: Richard A. Knox and Jane Meredith Adams, "AIDS Group Disrupts Sullivan Speech," *Boston Globe*, June 25, 1990.

187 **"into the system" and "None of this"**: Mark Harrington, "Let My People In," *OutWeek*, August 8, 1990.

188 **"We don't have" and "the boys"**: "Letters," *OutWeek*, August 22, 1990.

36. The Legacy of Ryan White

193 **"war zone"**: Thomas F. Sheridan, *Helping the Good Do Better: How a White Hat Lobbyist Advocates for Social Change* (Twelve, 2019), 10.

193 **"the infamous AIDS"**: Sheridan, *Helping the Good Do Better*, 23.

194 **"We don't spurn"**: Philip J. Hilts, "Bush, in First Address on AIDS, Backs a Bill to Protect Its Victims," *New York Times*, March 30, 1990.

195 **"Well, I'm not"**: Sheridan, *Helping the Good Do Better*, 36.

195 **"Jeanne, I know"**: Sheridan, *Helping the Good Do Better*, 39.

196 **"Every time ACT UP" and "turned off"**: Sheridan, *Helping the Good Do Better*, 43.

197 **"Should the president"**: Sheridan, *Helping the Good Do Better*, 48.

37. Women, Poor People, and Discrimination

198 **"Women were dying"**: Mireya Navarro, "Conversations: Katrina Haslip," *New York Times*, November 15, 1992.

200 **"How many women," "Women are dying," "One of the reasons"**: *United in Anger*, directed by Jim Hubbard, produced by Sarah Schulman and Jim Hubbard, 2012.

201 **"We recognize"**: "AIDS Activists Arrested," Associated Press article, October 3, 1990.

201 **"CDC, it's a disaster" and "They do nothing"**: "Second CDC Demonstration,

12/3/1990," video, *Women & AIDS*, actuporalhistory.org; and *United in Anger*, directed by Jim Hubbard, 2012.
201 **"continuing to look":** Elizabeth Coady, "300 Protest Definition of AIDS," *Atlanta Journal and Constitution*, December 4, 1990.
202 **"Errors of omission"** and **"Frankly, I can say":** Richard Knox, "Critics: Officials Ignored AIDS' First Signs Among Women," *Charlotte Observer*, December 18, 1990. This article is also the source of the data from California.

38. Wearing Red Ribbons
205 **"The East Village"** and **"We had no choice":** Nigel Wrench, "Why a Red Ribbon Means AIDS," BBC.com, November 7, 2003.
205 **"self-replicating":** Tom Geoghegan, "How a Red Ribbon Conquered the World," BBC.com, June 2, 2011.
206 **"Largely for symbolic":** Jesse Green, "The Year of the Ribbon," *New York Times*, May 3, 1992.
206 **"vibrant and attention-getting":** Wrench, "Why a Red Ribbon Means AIDS," November 7, 2003.
206 **"snowballed":** Geoghegan, "How a Red Ribbon Conquered the World," June 2, 2011.
207 **"because it was," "I wouldn't be,"** and **"I never want":** Green, "The Year of the Ribbon," May 3, 1992.

39. Ashes for the White House
209 **"Although he was":** Rachel Pepper, "With Knives, Whips or Chains," *Bay Area Reporter*, August 20, 1992.
209 **"I imagine":** David Wojnarowicz, *Close to the Knives: A Memoir of Disintegration* (Open Road, 2014), digital edition, location 1501.
209 **"we started":** Joy Episalla, interviewed by Sarah Schulman, December 6, 2003, ACT UP Oral History Project: A Program of MIX—The New York Lesbian & Gay Experimental Film Festival, Inc.
210 **"I think," "Bringing the ashes," "11 Years," "We're showing," "Act up," "Yesss,"** and **"Act up!":** "Ashes Action," video series, "Political Funerals," Act Up Oral History Project, actuporalhistory.org.
213 **"dropped the ball":** Philip J. Hilts, "Magic Johnson Quits Panel on AIDS," *New York Times*, September 26, 1992.
213 **"Do not go":** "Campaign '92: Transcript of the First Presidential Debate," *Washington Post*, October 11, 1992.

40. Victories Despite Death

214 **"I want to show"**: Mark Lowe Fisher, "Bury Me Furiously," "Political Funerals," actupny.org.

215 **"Mark Lowe Fisher," "It was Mark's," "Act up"**: "Mark Lowe Fisher Political Funeral," video, "Political Funerals," actuporalhistory.org.

216 **"czar"**: George Raine, "Clinton Vows War on AIDS," *San Francisco Examiner*, October 30, 1992.

216 **"I am" and "We have compelled"**: Navarro, "Conversations: Katrina Haslip," November 15, 1992.

217 **"So many women"**: Mireya Navarro, "More Cases and Fears Under Umbrella of AIDS," NY Times News Service, October 31, 1992.

41. One of the Bleakest Moments

222 **"It is one"**: Lawrence K. Altman, "Government Panel on H.I.V. Finds the Prospect for Treatment Bleak," *New York Times*, June 29, 1993.

222 **"This is a," "There is nothing," "Bill Clinton," and "We Will Not"**: "Tim Bailey Political Funeral," video series, "Political Funerals," Act Up Oral History Project, actuporalhistory.org.

224 **"I am getting," "Now, it is," "The treatments"**: Jeffrey Schmalz, "Whatever Happened to AIDS," *New York Times*, November 28, 1993.

225 **"I am frustrated" and "If you want"**: "Pedro Zamora Dies at 22," United Press International, November 17, 1994.

42. Shock and Awe

228 **"This is something"**: David France, *How to Survive a Plague*, 494–95.

228 **"People are not"**: Gina Kolata, "F.D.A. Debate on Speedy Access to AIDS Drugs Is Reopening," *New York Times*, September 12, 1994.

230 **"We can stop"**: France, *How to Survive a Plague*, 497.

231 **"What do you" and "Go home"**: Bill Bahlman, in discussion with the author, February 26, 2024.

231 **"We're seeing something" and "impressive"**: John Schwartz, "Three-Drug Treatment Shows Promise in Suppressing AIDS Virus," *Washington Post*, January 29, 1996.

231 **"We did it"**: France, *How to Survive a Plague*, 507.

232 **"mind-bogglingly"**: Larry Mass to Michael G. Long, email, February 24, 2024.

43. Undetectable

233 **"All of us"**: *How to Survive a Plague*, directed by David France, produced by David France and Howard Gertler, 2012.

NOTES

233 **"On paper"**: "The End of AIDS?" *Newsweek*, December 1, 1996.
233 **"Lazarus effect"**: *How to Survive a Plague*, directed by David France, 2012.
234 **"Lazarus, come out!"**: John 11: 43-44, *The New Oxford Annotated Bible with Apocrypha: New Revised Standard Version* (Oxford University Press, 2018).
234 **"melting back"**: *How to Survive a Plague*, directed by David France, produced by David France and Howard Gertler, 2012.
234 **"No obits"**: Timothy Rodrigues, "No obits," *Bay Area Reporter*, August 13, 1998. Ann Bausum's wonderful book, *Viral*, also cites this article in her conclusion.
234 **"Wow"**: Mary Curtius, "S.F. Paper's Brief Headline Signals a Moment to Rejoice," *Los Angeles Times*, August 15, 1998.
234 **"We all deserve"**: Rodrigues, "No obits," August 13, 1998.
235 **"The BAR"**: Curtius, "S.F. Paper's Brief Headline Signals a Moment to Rejoice," August 15, 1998.
236 **"For that to happen"** and **"See you around"**: "Death Takes a Holiday," *Bay Area Reporter*, August 13, 1998.

Epilogue

237 **"I plan on"**: Earvin "Magic" Johnson, press conference comments, November 7, 1991, Los Angeles, California. CNN has posted a video of these comments online at "Magic Johnson HIV Announcement Part I," 9:30, https://www.youtube.com/watch?v=VbdOQUARrEU.
237 **"HIV was a death"**: Cindy Augustine, "Earvin 'Magic' Johnson on the 1992 Olympic Dream Team: 'It Was the Best Moment of My Life,'" BBC.com, June 24, 2024, https://www.bbc.com/worklife/article/20240621-magic-johnson-interview-influential-katty-kay.
239 **"turn the tide"**: Thomas P. Sheehy, "PEPFAR's Legacy 20 Years On," USIP.org, March 8, 2023, https://www.usip.org/publications/2023/03/pepfars-profound-legacy-20-years.

IMAGE CREDITS

- xiii ACT UP New York Records, Manuscript and Archives Division, The New York Public Library
- 5 Gran Fury Collection, Manuscripts and Archives Division, The New York Public Library
- 6 Gran Fury Collection, Manuscripts and Archives Division, The New York Public Library
- 9 New York Daily News Archive/Getty Images
- 13 Photo by Diana Jo Davies, Manuscript and Archives Division, The New York Public Library
- 17 Perry Brass
- 21 ACT UP New York Records, Manuscripts and Archives Division, The New York Public Library
- 29 From the personal photo collection of Lawrence D. Mass
- 32 New York Times/PARS International
- 39 Gran Fury Collection, Manuscripts and Archives Division, The New York Public Library
- 43 © Roger Ressmeyer/CORBIS/VCG via Getty Images
- 44 Rink Foto
- 48 Shanti Project Records, Courtesy of Gay, Lesbian, Bisexual, Transgender Historical Society
- 53 Don Hogan Charles/The New York Times/Redux
- 61 Richard Dworkin
- 69 Gran Fury Collections, Manuscripts and Archives Division, The New York Public Library
- 74 Lee Snider Photograph Collection, Fales Library and Special Collections, New York University
- 77 National Gay and Lesbian Task Force records, #7301. Division of Rare and Manuscript Collections, Cornell University Library.
- 83 Shanti Project Records, Courtesy of Gay, Lesbian, Bisexual, Transgender Historical Society
- 87 © Ilka Hartmann, 2024
- 93 San Francisco Chronicle/Hearst Newspapers via Getty Images
- 94 Gran Fury Collection, Manuscripts and Archives Division, The New York Public Library

IMAGE CREDITS

- 98 Reagan White House Photographs, National Archives
- 103 Courtesy of the Kokomo Tribune
- 110 Steve Ringman/San Francisco Chronicle/Polaris
- 119 ACT UP New York Records, The New York Public Library
- 130 Bill Bahlman
- 137 Archives and Manuscripts Division, The New York Public Library
- 140 Catherine McGann/Getty Images
- 144 John Sotomayor/The New York Times/Redux
- 147 Gran Fury Collection, Manuscripts and Archives Division, The New York Public Library
- 150 Liz Hafalia/San Francisco Chronicle/Polaris Images
- 153 Courtesy of The National AIDS Memorial
- 156 The J. Paul Getty Museum, Los Angeles, © JEB (Joan E. Biren)
- 160 Associated Press
- 167 ACT UP New York Records, Manuscripts and Archives Division, The New York Public Library
- 172 Mikki Ansin/Getty Images
- 182 AP Images
- 186 © Rick Gerharter
- 191 Gran Fury Collection, Manuscripts and Archives Division, The New York Public Library
- 200 © Donna Binder and *Nothing Without Us* (dir. Harriet Hirshorn), a Women Make Movies release
- 203 ACT UP New York Records, Manuscripts and Archives Division, The New York Public Library
- 207 Visual AIDS Artist Caucus
- 212 © Meg Handler
- 215 Stephen Barker
- 219 ACT UP New York Records, Manuscripts and Archives Division, The New York Public Library
- 223 © Donna Binder
- 226 Rick Gerharter
- 229 Rich Wandel
- 235 Bay Area Reporter
- 238 Ilka Hartmann

INDEX

Page numbers in italic indicate illustrations.

Abbott Laboratories, 230, 231
ABC, 79
abstinence, 162, 225
ACT UP; *See also* Kramer, Larry
   and Bill Bahlman, 228, *229*
   at Tim Bailey funeral, 222–24
   and George H. W. Bush, 213–16
   and CARE bill, 196, 197
   and CDC definition of AIDS, 217
   at FDA (1988), 169–73
   at International AIDS Conference (1990), 184–87, *186–87*
   and Lavender Hill Mob, 162
   and the Marys, 209, 214
   at National March on Washington (1987), 154, 157
   and needle exchanges, 177
   at NIH (1990), 179–81, *182–83*
   posters, *21–22*, *69*, *119–20*, *167–68*, *203*, *219–20*
   and red ribbon campaign, 207–8
   scattering of AIDS victims' ashes by, 210–12, *212*
   and T+D committee, 180, 188–89
   and Treatment Action Group, 228
   Wall Street protests, 142–44, *144–45*, 175–77
   at White House protest (1987), 156
ACT UP Los Angeles, 171
ACT UP New York, *13–14*, 169–70, 173, 175, 184, 188–89, 199–200, 222
ACT UP San Francisco, 210, 235
aerosol pentamidine, 173
Africa, 239, 240
AIDS (acquired immune deficiency syndrome); *See also* HIV (human immunodeficiency virus); people with AIDS (PWAs)
   about, 2
   and George H.W. Bush administration, 194–97
   CDC and, 58, 216

and Clinton administration, 221–22, 224, 225
deaths from, 88, 112, 222, 224, 231, 240
discovery of cause of, 85–86
Jerry Falwell on, 84–85
first use of term, 58
government definition of, 199
Larry Kramer on, 70–71
public health efforts, 161–62
and Reagan administration, 65–66, 73, 99–101, 105–6, 161–65
search for drug treatments, 98–99, 169, 227
vaccine for prevention of, 86
women with, 198–202, *203*, 204
AIDS Alliance, 75, 76
AIDS Counseling and Education Program (Bedford Hills Correctional Facility), 198
"AIDSGATE" (poster), *147–48*
AIDS Network, 72
AIDS Project Los Angeles, 108
AIDS Quilt, 149–54, *150*, *153*, 157, 210
AIDS wards, 80–82, 193
AL 721 (AIDS drug), 123–27, 154
alternative therapies, 127
Altman, Lawrence K., 222, 224
American Foundation for AIDS Research (amfAR), 108, 132
American Red Cross, 116
Americans with Disabilities Act (ADA), 196
anal intercourse, 14, 35, 36, 62, 90, 92, 157
antidiscrimination laws, 33, 36, 164, 194, 196, 216
antiretroviral therapy (ART), 233–34
Apuzzo, Virginia, 157
ashes, scattering of AIDS victims', 210–12, *212*
Associated Press, 176
Atlanta, Ga., 129, 141, 201
Aucoin, Doug, 31
Aurigemma, Mark, 143–44
AZT, *119–20*, 121–23, 125, 142, 143, 170–72, 175–77, 179–81, 222, 227, 230, 231

INDEX

bacterial pneumonia, 27, 199, 216; *See also* pneumocystis pneumonia (PCP)
Badlands (Washington, DC, nightclub), 97, 98
Bahlman, Bill, 131, 132, 162, 228–30, *229*, 232
Bailey, Tim, 222–24, *223*
Bailey House, 139
Baker, Gilbert, 112, 114
Barr, David, 170
Barré-Sinoussi, Françoise, 86
bathhouses, closing of, 90–93, *93*
Bauer, Jamie, 128–29, 222, 223
Bay Area Reporter, 234–36, *235*
Bedford Hills Correctional Facility, 198
Berkowitz, Richard, 59–62, *61*, 76
   How to Have Sex in an Epidemic: One Approach, 61–62
Bethesda, Md., 117, 180–81, *182–83*
Beth Israel Hospital (New York City), 23–25
Black people, 73, 156, 181, 182, 202, 211, 237, 240
Blake, Robert, 152
bleach, 177
Block, Alice, 15
blood drives, 116
"BLOOD ON ITS HANDS" (poster), *191–92*
Blood Sisters, 116, 117
blood transfusions, 86, 103, 104, 115
Bohrer, Steven, 142
Bordowitz, Greg, 169–70
Borg, Björn, 31
Boston, Mass., 18
Brass, Perry, 12–16, 18, 19, 50, 90
Broadway theater industry, 205
Bronx, N.Y., 52
Bronx Lebanon Hospital, 52
Brugiere, Frederic, 86
Buckley, William F., Jr., 128, 135
buddy program, 51–52
Burke, Ronnie, 235
Burroughs Wellcome, 175–77, *176*, 177, 179
Bush, Barbara, 195, 213
Bush, George H. W., and administration, *167–68*, 186, 194–97, 207, 210–13, 215, 216
Bush, George W., and administration, 239
buyers' clubs, 125–26, 169

California, 202
Callen, Michael, 59–62, *61*, 76, 78, 125, 126
   How to Have Sex in an Epidemic: One Approach, 61–62
Campbell, Bobbi, 41–45, *43*, 46–49, 62, 72, 74–76, 78, 88–89, 112
Capitol building (Washington, DC), 222
Castro district (San Francisco), *44*, 44–46, 72–73, 87, 92, 111–14, 151
CD4 cells, 122, 174, 216, 230, 234
Centers for Disease Control and Prevention (CDC), 1–3, 31, 55–58, 65, 98, 105, 106, 129, 131, 136, 199–202, *200*, 204, 216, 217
Central Park (New York City), 18
Chaikin, Lu, 85
Cher, 107
Chicago, Ill., 18, 170
Cicero, Ind., 159
clinical drug trials, 121–23, 125, 163, 164, 169–74, 179, 181, 182, 227, 228, 230, 231, 233
Clinton, Bill, and administration, 212, 216, 221–22, 224, 225
Close to the Knives (Wojnarowicz), 209
CNN, 132
Coalition for Lesbian and Gay Rights, 140
Collart, Yanou, 100
combination therapy, 234, 237
Committee United Against Violence, 149
Community Research Initiative, 164
Conant, Marcus, 26, 42, 56, 88, 90–92
condoms, 15–16, 18, 36, *39–40*, 60–62, 155, 162, 177, 187, 216, 225
Conference on Retroviruses and Opportunistic Infections, 231
Congress, 101, 193–94, 217, 225, 239
Cook, Tony, 159, 160
Cordova, Ronald, 151
Cox, Spencer, 230, 231
Crixivan, 229–32, 232
Crossfire (news program), 132
cytomegalovirus (CMV), 24, 59

Day, Doris, 99
de la Cruz, Iris, 201
Delaney, Martin, 228
Delta Queens, 171
"DEMAND AN AIDS CURE NOW" (poster), *219–20*
Democratic National Convention (1984), 87

INDEX

Democratic Party, 87, 91
demonstrations and protests, 141, 200; *See also* ACT UP; marches
    CDC conference (Atlanta, 1987), 129–32
    International AIDS Conference (Munich, 2024), 240–41
    National Lesbian and Gay Health Conference (Denver, 1983), 76–78
    Stonewall protests, 5–6, 7–12, *9*, 12, 129
    Wall Street, 142–44, *144–45*, 175–77
Denmark, David, 81
Denver, Colo., 76–78, *77*
"Denver Principles," 78
Department of Health and Human Services, 85–86, 101, 109, 110, *110*, 115, 186, 200, *200*
dextran sulfate, 171
die-ins, 181, 200
discrimination, 65, 114, 117, 131, 163, 164, 185, 194, 216, 240; *See also* antidiscrimination laws; homophobia
diseases, syndromes vs., 56–57
Dormont, Dominique, 99, 100
Dorow, Heidi, 188
Dowdle, Walter, 132
Downs, Larry, 27
drug runners, 127, 169
drug treatments, 99, 227–36; *See also* AZT
drug trials, *See* clinical drug trials
drug users, 28, 57, 58, 104, 135, 154, 163, 170, 182, 199, 217
Durant, Joseph, 111, 112, 150, 151
Dynasty (TV show), 99, 107

Ebreo, Lenny, 15, 16
Eckington, Sally, 157, 158
Edwards, Mary Jane, 152
Eigo, Jim, 173, 174
Emini, Emilio, 231
"ENJOY AZT" (poster), *119–20*
Episalla, Joy, 209–10, 214, 222–24
Evans, Linda, 99, 107–8

Fader, Michael, 10
Falwell, Jerry, 84–85, 89, 162
Fauci, Anthony, 126–27, 174, 177, 183, 202, 204
Feldman, Mark, 73, 75, 150–52
Feldman, Marvin, 152

Fifth National Lesbian and Gay Health Conference (Denver, 1983), 76–78, *77*
"FIGHT AIDS" (poster), *xiii–xiv*
Finkelstein, Avram, 134–36, 138, 140, 207
Fisher, Mark Lowe, 214–16, *215*
Food and Drug Administration (FDA), 115, 116, 123, 125, 129, 136, 141–43, 162, 169–74, *172*, 177, 227, 228, 232, 239
Forbes magazine, 33
Frame, Allen, 205
France, 86, 100
France, David, 33, 62, 79–80
Francis, Donald, 173
Franke-Ruta, Garance, 183, 228
Franks, Bert, 109
Fried, Richard Bruce, 153
Fried, Suzanne, 153
Friedman-Kien, Alvin, 26, 34, 36, 42
fundraising efforts, 35, 37, 64, 74, 107–8, 125, 194

Gallo, Robert, 85–86
Garcia, Angel, 73, 74
Garcia, Robert, 170
Garden Grove, Calif., 116
Gay and Lesbian Alliance Against Defamation (GLAAD), 128–29
Gay and Lesbian Center (Garden Grove, Calif.), 116–17
"Gay Cancer" poster, 44, *44*, 45
Gay Liberation Front (GLF), 12, *13*
gay men's health clinics, 16–18
Gay Men's Health Crisis (GMHC), 50–55, *53*, 64, 65, 80, 86, 127, 132, 139, 141, 142, 196, 205, 232, 240
Gay Men's Health Project, *17*, 18, 19, 23–25, 28, 50, 90
Gaynor, Gloria, 42
Geary, Jim, 46, 84, 85
Gebbie, Kristine, 221–22
Gefter, Philip, 33
gender roles, 14
genital herpes, 24
Germany, 128
Gilead Sciences, 241
Goldberg, Whoopi, 107, 157
gonorrhea, 13–14
Gottlieb, Michael, 98–99, 107
Gran Fury, 5–6, *39–40*, *95–96*, *191–92*

267

INDEX

Gray, Hillel, 158
Greenwich Village, 7–11, 14, 15, 28, 34, 52, 58, 62–63, 126, 133–35, 138, 139, 214
GRID (Gay-Related Immune Deficiency), 57
Guidelines and Recommendations for Healthful Gay Sexual Activity, 62

Haiti and Haitians, 57, 58
Hamilton Heights High School (Cicero, Ind.), 159–61
Hannan, Tom, 125
Harrington, Mark, 177–80, 187–88, 234
Harvey Milk Lesbian/Gay Democratic Club, 91
Harvey Milk Plaza (San Francisco), 92
Haslip, Katrina, 197–99, 216–17
Hatch, Orrin, 193–95, 195
Heckler, Margaret, 85–86, 101, 115
hemophilia, 58, 104
herpes, 24
Hilliard, Bobby, 88
Hispanic people, 156, 182, 240
HIV (human immunodeficiency virus)
 about, 1–2
 AL 721 and, 124, 125
 antiretroviral therapy for treatment of, 233–34
 AZT and, 121, 122, 175, 222, 231
 and blood transfusions, 115, 157
 and CDC definition of AIDS, 217
 Crixivan and, 229, 231
 current status of, 239–41
 discovery of, 86
 discrimination against people infected with, 184, 185, 187, 216
 educational campaigns about, 162–64, 221, 225, 226
 and Rock Hudson, 99, 108
 and immigrant bans, 184, 185, 216
 and Magic Johnson, 212, 237
 and needle exchange programs, 177
 origins of, 3
 Presidential Commission on, 155, 159
 and protease inhibitors, 183, 228
 Retrovir and, 230
 testing for, 129–31, 155
 transmission of, 2, 103–5, 158
 women with, 187, 188, 198–200, 202
Hoffman-La Roche, 227–28

Hollywood, 107
Holocaust, 128, 138
homophobia, 79, 80, 109–11, 116–17, 171; *See also* discrimination
homosexuality, attempts to "cure" people of, 85
Horst, Ian, 79
Hoth, Daniel, 181, 202, 204
Houston, Tex., 170
Hoven, Judith, 202
Howard, Brian, 134
How to Have Sex in an Epidemic: One Approach (Callen and Berkowitz), 61–62
HPA-23, 99
Hudson, Rock, 97–101, *98*, 107–9, 153, 194
Human Rights Campaign Fund, 157
Humm, Andy, 36, 139–40
Hundt, John, 109
hydrogen peroxide, 127

immigrants and immigration, 185, 216
Immigration and Naturalization Service (INS), 185
immune system, 23–25, 29–31, 49, 56, 59–60, 107, 121, 122
International AIDS Conference (Munich, 2024), 240–41
International AIDS Conference (San Francisco, 1990), 184–87, *186–87*
Irons, Jeremy, 205
Israel, 123, 124
"I Will Survive" (Gloria Gaynor song), 42

Jewish people, 30, 128
John, Elton, 195
Johnson, Earvin "Magic," Jr., 212–13, 237, 238
Johnston, Oliver, 134
Jones, Cleve, 111–14, 123, 144, 149–52, *150*, 154

Kaposi's sarcoma (KS), 25–26, 31–33, 35–37, 41–47, *47*, 49, 56, 57, 72, 79, 98, 234
Kennedy, Ted, 193–95
King, Gwendolyn, 201
Kinsolving, Lester, 65–66
"KISSING DOESN'T KILL" (poster), *94–96*
Kokomo, Ind., 102, *103*, 159

Kokomo Tribune, 103
Koop, C. Everett, 161–62
Kramer, Larry, 35–37, 50, 64–66, 71–72, 75, 126–27, 132–33, 139–41, *140,* 143, 232
  The Normal Heart, 139
Kraus, Bill, 91
Kreloff, Charles, 134
Krim, Mathilde, 132

Lambda Legal, 194
Laubenstein, Linda, 26
Lavender Hill Mob, 129–33, *130,* 139, 141, 162, *229*
"Lazarus effect," 233–34
legislation, 36, 116–17, 193–97, 216, 239
Lesbian and Gay Community Center (New York City), 139
lesbians, 8, 15, 63, 76, 114, 116–17, 142, 157
Liberace, 153
Liberation House, 15, 16
Lione, Chris, 134, 135
Littlejohn, Larry, 91
Long, Iris, 169
Los Angeles, Calif., 18, 31, 101, 107, 108, 171, 194, 197
Los Angeles Lakers, 237
Los Angeles Times, 116
lymph glands (lymph nodes), 24, 25, 32, 86
lymphoma, 46
Lynchburg, Va., 85

Magee, Mary, 81, 82
mandatory testing, 131, 155
marches; *See also* demonstrations and protests
  candlelight march (San Francisco, 1985), 111–14
  National March for Lesbian/Gay Rights (1984), 87, *87,* 88
  National March on Washington for Lesbian and Gay Rights (1987), 154–58, *156*
Marcus, Eric, 31–33
Marez, Dave, 72–74
Marys, the, 209–10, 214
Mass, Larry, 27–30, *29,* 35–36, 50, 232
masturbation, mutual, 61
May, Michael, 124, 126
McFarlane, Rodger, 51, 80, 205, 208
McGovern, Theresa, 198–200, 217
Meckler, Gary, 126

media coverage, 31–32, *32,* 79, 132, 154, 172, 183; *See also specific media, e.g.:* New York Times
Medicaid, 65, 201
Merck & Co., 229–31
Mexico, 127
Mildvan, Donna, 23–25
military, gays and lesbians in the, 221
Milk, Harvey, 111, 112
Miller, Mark, 98, 100
Miskoff Theater (New York City), 205
Moed Paolerico, Alison, 81
Montagnier, Luc, 86
Moore, Frank, 205, 206
Moral Majority, 84
Morbidity and Mortality Weekly Report, 31
Morgan, Tracey, 188
Morrison, Cliff, 80–82
Moscone, George, 111, 112
Moscone Center (San Francisco), 87, 88, 185
Moskowitz, Hal, 52–55
Mothers Against Drunk Driving, 205
Mothers of AIDS Patients, 152
Mount Sinai Hospital (New York City), 51
MTV, 225
Munich, Germany, 240
mutual masturbation, 61

National AIDS Brigade, 177
National AIDS Research Foundation, 108
National Association of People with AIDS, 78
National Cancer Institute (NCI), 85–86, 117, 121
National Coalition of Gay STD Services, 62
National Coalition on AIDS conference, 194
National Commission on AIDS, 212–13
National Conference on Women and HIV Infection, 202
National Institute of Allergy and Infectious Diseases (NIAID), 126, 129, 204
National Institutes of Health (NIH), 126, 129, *167–68,* 169, 173, 174, 178–83, *182–83,* 185, 187–88, 202, 217, 222, 228
National Mall (Washington, DC), 151, 152, *153,* 210
National March for Lesbian/Gay Rights (1984), 87, *87,* 88
National March on Washington for Lesbian and Gay Rights (1987), 154–58, *156*

National Review, 128
Nazis, 128, 131, 132, 149
New Wave movement, 136
New York City; *See also* Greenwich Village
   ACT UP in, *13–14*, 169–70, 173, 175, 184, 188–89, 199–200, 222
   candlelight march (1983), *74*
   Community Research Initiative in, 164
   emergence of AIDS in, 26–34, 37, 41, 56
   Mark Fisher funeral protest in, 214–16, *215*
   Gay Men's Health Crisis in, 196, 240
   homophobia in, 80
   Lavender Hill Mob in, 129–33, *130*, 139
   the Marys in, 209–10, 214
   National AIDS Brigade in, 177
   PWA movement in, 78, 135, 156
   red ribbon campaign in, 205–6
   "SILENCE = DEATH" campaign in, 134–36, *137*, 138, 143
   Stonewall protests, 5–6, 7–12, *9*, 12, 129
   targeting of gay baths and hangouts in, 13, 18
   Wall Street protests, 142–44, *144–45*, 175–77
   women with AIDS in, 198, 216
New York City Department of Health and Mental Hygiene, 18, 28
New York Daily News, 124
New York Native, 27–30, 37, 59, 71–72
New York Police Department (NYPD), 8
New York Stock Exchange (NYSE), 142, 175–76
New York Times, 31–32, *32*, 57, 132, 139, 207, 222, 224
New York University Medical Center, 26, 34, 51
Nixon, Richard, and administration, 105, 156
Normal Heart, The (Kramer), 139
Northop, Ann, 207–8

Oakland, Calif., 157
O'Brien, John, 9, 10
O'Connell, Patrick, 205–6
Olson, Dale, 107
Olympic Games (2024), 237
opportunistic infections, 31, 56–58, 179, 187, 234
Orange County, Calif., 116, 117
Ortleb, Chuck, 30

Our Bodies, Ourselves, 16
OutWeek, 187

Paris, France, 86, 100
Parker, Jon C., 177–78
Pasteur Institute, 99
Patient Constituency Working Group, 179–80, 187
pentamidine, 173
People magazine, 151
people who injected drugs (PIDs), 177
people with AIDS (PWAs), 2, 74–78, 80–83, 88, 104, 115, 131, 135, 156, 171, 188–89, 199, 217, 238
People with AIDS Health Group, 125–26
PEP (post-exposure prophylaxis), 2
Pepper, Rachel, 209
Percy military hospital, 99, 100
Perez, Eric, 129, 130
Persian Gulf War, 205
Petrelis, Michael, 129–32, 139, 142
Phillips, Steven, 28
Pine, Seymour, 7
pink triangle symbol, 128, 129, 136, *137*, 138
placebos, 122, 174, 230
Play Fair! (brochure), 62
pneumocystis pneumonia (PCP), 24, 25, 30, 31, 43, 54, 56, 121, 122, 173, 199
Praxis Pharmaceuticals, 154
prejudice, *See* discrimination; homophobia
PrEP, 2, 240
Presidential Commission on the Human Immunodeficiency Virus Epidemic, 155, 159
President's Emergency Plan for AIDS Relief (PEPFAR), 239
Pride Week, 151
promiscuity, 36, 59–61
protease inhibitors, 183, 227–28, 230

Rabinowitz, Marc, 16
Rafuse, Joseph, 121
Ramble, the (location in NY's Central Park), 18
Ramsauer, Ken, 79, 80
"Rare Cancer Seen in 41 Homosexuals" (*New York Times* article), 31–32, *32*
Ray brothers, 157
"READ MY LIPS" (poster), *69–70*

INDEX

Reagan, Nancy, 97, 98, *98*, 100
Reagan, Ronald, and administration, 63, 65–66, 73, 97, *98*, 100, 101, 105–6, 108, *130*, 136, *147–48*, 155–57, 161–65, 171
Real World, The (reality show), 225
red ribbons, 205–8
Retrovir, 230, 232
reverse transcriptase, 121
Reynolds, Burt, 108
Rhode Island, 150
Rich, Frank, 139
"RIOT" (Gran Fury painting), *5–6*
Rivera, Geraldo, 79
Roach, Stephen, 125, 154
Robinson, David, 210, 211
Robinson, Marty, 129–31
Rockett, Rita, 82
Rockville, Md., 170, 172
Rodwell, Craig, 10–11
Roosevelt Hospital (New York City), 216
Russell, Steve, 109
Russo, Vito, 171
Ryan White Comprehensive AIDS Resources Emergency (CARE) Act, 195–97, 216, 239

Sacramento, Calif., 149
Sacramento Bee, 149
safe sex, 62, 63, 76, 78, 88
St. Mark's Clinic (New York City), 14
St. Vincent's Hospital (New York City), 27
San Diego, Calif., 116
San Francisco, Calif.; *See also* Castro district
   ACT UP in, 170, 210, 235
   AIDS Alliance in, 75, 76
   AIDS Quilt idea developed in, 149
   "bathhouse battles" in, 90–93, *93*
   buyers' clubs in, 126
   candlelight marches in, 72–74, 111–14
   emergence of AIDS in, 26, 41–45, 56
   Health and Human Services protest in, 109, *110*
   National March for Lesbian/Gay Rights in, 87, *87*, 88
   Sisters of Perpetual Indulgence in, 62, 74
   Sixth International AIDS Conference held in, 184–87, *186–87*
   Trilingual AIDS Hotline in, *238*
San Francisco AIDS Foundation, 234, 240

San Francisco Chronicle, 108
San Francisco Community Consortium, 173
San Francisco General Hospital, 80–82, *83*, 88, 193, 202
San Francisco Sentinel, 42–43, 47
Schell, Randy, 149
Schietinger, Helen, 76
Schmalz, Jeffrey, 224
Segal, Mark, 7, 8, 10, 87
sexually transmitted diseases (STDs), 13–16, 18, 24, 56, 59, 62, 162
sex workers, 28, 54, 59, 60
Shanti Project, 43, 46, *48*, 84
Shapiro, Vivian, 142
Sharpe, Phyllis, 182, 201
Sheehy, Thomas, 239
Sheridan, Thomas, 193, 195–97
Shilts, Randy, 108
shingles, 25, 41
"SILENCE = DEATH," 134–36, *137*, 138, 143, *147–48*, 156, 157, 171, 207
Silverman, Mervyn, 90–92
Sisters of Perpetual Indulgence, 62, 74
Sixth International AIDS Conference (San Francisco, 1990), 184–87, *186–87*
Smith, Michael, 151
Smith, Stuart, 116–17
Socarrás, Jorge, 134
Social Security Administration (SSA), 199, 200, 201, 217
Sonnabend, Joseph, 58–60, 125
Speakes, Larry, 65–66
Spindler, Benjamin, 116–17
Staley, Peter, 171, 175, 181, 184, 185, 222, 233
Stonewall protests, *5–6*, 7–12, *9*, 12, 129
"STORM THE NIH" (poster), *167–68*
Sullivan, Louis W., 186, 187
Summer Olympics (2024), 237
Supreme Court, 157
Sweeney, Tim, 142
Swift and Terrible Retribution Committee, 128–29
syndromes, diseases vs., 56–57

tattooing, proposals for forced, 128, 135
Taylor, Elizabeth, 107, 108, 194
testing, mandatory, 131, 155
Tombstoners, 171, *172*
Tony Awards, 205

INDEX

Traci (transgender person), 53–55
transmission, 2, 36, 49, 60, 61, 81, 90, 103–5, 160, 198; *See also* sexually transmitted diseases (STDs)
Treatment Action Group (TAG), 188, 217, 222, 227–28, 230
Treatment and Data Committee (T+D), 169, 177, 180, 183, 184, 188–89
Trilingual AIDS Hotline, *238*
Truax, Brad, 116
Trucks, the (location in NY's Central Park), 18
Trummer, Mike, 153

UNAIDS, 239
Understanding AIDS (booklet), 162
United Nations, 239
United States Institute of Peace, 239
University of California, Los Angeles, 107
University of California, San Francisco, 42, 76
"USE CONDOMS" (poster), *39–40*

vaccines, 86
Van Gorder, Dana, 234
Vassar College, 31
Vick, Barbara, 116
Vietnam War, 158
Viola, Tom, 205
Visual AIDS Artists Caucus, 205–6, *207*

Wallace, Joyce, 27–28
Wall Street protests, 142–44, *144–45*, 175–77
Walsh, Gary, 72, 74, 75, 84–86, 112

Walt Disney Productions, 153
Ward 5B (San Francisco General Hospital), 80–82, *83*, 193
Washington, DC, 97, 151, 152, *153*, 193, 195, 200, *200*, 209–10, 222, *223*; *See also* National March on Washington for Lesbian and Gay Rights
Washington Post, 172, 183
Watkins, James, 161–65
Waxman, Henry, 101
Weiss, Ted, 101
Wellikoff, Rick, 26
"WE'RE FIRED UP" (poster), *21–22*
White, Jeanne, 104, 159, 195–97
White, Ryan, 101–6, *103*, 115, 159–61, *160*, 195–96
White House (Washington, DC), 65–66, 97, 98, *98*, 155–57, 197, 209–11, *212*, 222, 223
William, Dan, 18, 19, 25, 28, 41, 56
Wisotzy, Paul, 234
Wojnarowicz, David, *Close to the Knives*, 209
Wolf, Ed, 44, 45
women, 16, 156, 171, 181, 187–88, 198–202, *200*, *203*, 204, 217, 240; *See also* lesbians
Women's Caucus and Majority Action Committee (ACT UP), 171
Wonder, Roy L., 92, 93
Wonder, Stevie, 107

Young, Ralph, 143

Zamora, Pedro, 225, 226, *226*
Ziegler, John, 184, 185